D1526441

Spiritual Liberation
and Human Freedom
in Contemporary Asia

The Rockwell Lecture Series

Niels Nielsen and Werner Kelber
General Editors

Vol. 1

PETER LANG
New York • Bern • Frankfurt am Main • Paris

Joseph Mitsuo Kitagawa

Spiritual Liberation and Human Freedom in Contemporary Asia

PETER LANG
New York • Bern • Frankfurt am Main • Paris

Library of Congress Cataloging-in-Publication Data

Kitagawa, Joseph Mitsuo
    Spiritual liberation and human freedom in
contemporary Asia / Joseph Mitsuo Kitagawa.
        p. cm. — (The Rockwell lecture series ; Vol. 1)
    Lectures delivered at Rice University in 1977.
    Includes bibliographical references and index.
        1. East Asia—Religion.   2. Religion and culture—East
Asia.   3. Religions—Relations.   4. East and West.
I. Title. II. Series.
BL1055.K57   1990   291'.095'0904—dc20   90-38367
ISBN 0-8204-1318-6   CIP
ISSN 0-1052-2204

© Peter Lang Publishing, Inc., New York 1990

Printed in the United States of America.

In memory of my brothers

Chiaki

and

Daisuke

Table of Contents

Preface ix

Introduction 1

Chapter 1   The Eastern "World of Meaning" 23

Chapter 2   Mutual Image: European and Asian 55

Chapter 3   Revolution and Tradition 87

Chapter 4   Spiritual Liberation and Freedom in Asia 115

Appendix 1   Some Remarks on Buddhism 165

Appendix 2   Religious Visions of the End of the World 179

Bibliography 193

Preface

The present volume is based on the 1977 Rockwell Lectures delivered at Rice University, Houston, Texas. Still today I have many fond memories of my time on the Rice Campus--the interesting discussions and conversations I carried on with students, the warm friendship extended to me by faculty colleagues at Rice and the University of Houston, and especially the thoughtfulness of Professor Niels C. Nielsen, Jr. of Rice, who had invited me and also looked after me during my stay. Although the appearance of the book has been delayed for a decade, due in large part to my prolonged illness and slow recovery, the intervening years have given me time to think more about the current religious situation in Asia, the theme of my Rockwell Lectures. I realize, of course, that the vastness of the topic is such that no one person can adequately deal with it. The best I can do under the circumstances is offer my personal essays or reflections on this fascinating subject, based on my limited knowledge and personal acquaintance with it.

Probably the best way to explain my own concerns with the subject of this volume is to give a brief autobiographical account in the Introduction. Readers will see that understanding contemporary Asia is for me both a scholarly and existential necessity. I have of course discussed many facets of this problem elsewhere on many occasions, but I am particularly grateful to Rice University for giving me the opportunity to systematically present my reflections on the subject.

As readers can readily gather from the Introduction below, my upbringing in Asia and my residence on this side of the ocean for now well over four decades has made me naturally very sensitive to the need for mutual understanding between the East and the West. I am also grateful that the Rockefeller Foundation, the Social Science Research Council, the International Council of Philosophy and Humanistic Studies, the Japan Society for the Promotion of Science, the Chinese Academy of Science, the Divinity School and Center for Far Eastern Studies of the University of Chicago, and many other groups and institutions have made it possible for me to travel frequently to many parts of Asia. Throughout my life, I have learned about Asia, Asians, and Asian traditions through, as we often say, "reading, seeing, and meeting." I literally do not know how to thank all those people on both sides of the ocean who have enlightened me in numerous ways. I should express my special sense of indebtedness to my wife, Evelyn, and our daughter, Anne Rose, as well as my colleagues both in the Divinity School and the Department of East Asian Languages and Civilizations of the University of Chicago, who always stood by me in my modest effort to interpret the East to the West, and vice versa.

Specifically in reference to this volume, I owe a great deal to Professor Nielsen of Rice University for his patience beyond the call of duty for waiting all these years. It was he who also made arrangement with Peter Lang Publishing to process this book. Of course, I would be remiss if I failed to thank Ms. Stephanie Paulsell and Ms. Nathelda McGee for typing my manuscript, and Ms. Jane Geaney, Mr. Jeffrey Kripal, and Ms. Karen Pechilis, whose careful editing of the typescript resulted in many improvements. Also as in many other things since my illness, I have depended heavily on my friend and former research assistant, Mr. Peter Chemery, for various substantial and tedious chores connected with the present volume.

While writing this manuscript, I often thought of my brothers and wished I could have discussed many ideas with them as I used to do. Alas! One of them died in Tokyo, and the other in Switzerland. Like our parents, they too lived in a turbulent era, but they managed to live with their virtues of integrity, honesty and unshakable faith in the future of humankind and the world. Thus, to their memories this volume is humbly dedicated.

J.M.K.

Introduction

The longer I live, the more convinced I am about the correctness of Santayana's famous dictum that those who refuse to learn from history are condemned to repeat the mistakes of the past. I take it that what Santayana had in mind was not only our "memories" of the past but our efforts to "interpret" the meaning of the past. To be sure, both our memories and our interpretations are far from perfect, partly because we are not always conscious of all the pertinent factors involved and also because we are not aware of what lies in store for us most of the time. Moreover, our memories are not simply our own individual possessions; they are part of the corporate memories of our families, our generations, our cultural and ethnic groups, and our human race. Unfortunately, there is no single vantage point from which to assess memories or interpretations of the past. Yet we must make every effort to recall the past and what we have done as individuals and as corporate beings, so that our undertakings in turn will become available as data for the memories of future generations.

Our family record shows that my father, Kitagawa Chiyokichi, was born before the restoration of imperial rule (A.D. 1867) from the feudal regime of the Tokugawa family in the Akaho district, not far from the city of Himeji in the present Hyōgo prefecture, made famous by the forty-seven retainers who, in their loyalty to their feudal lord, avenged his humiliation. My father had a thorough training in Confucian—or what we now call Neo-Confucian—learning. Evidently, Buddhism was not strong in the Akaho district and he was not steeped in the Buddhist tradition as were some of his contemporaries. After spending a few years teaching grammar school, he decided to go to Tokyo, the new national capital. With the exception of the short ride on the train between Yokohama and Tokyo, he walked the entire distance,

following the historic Tōkaidō highway. I was born in 1915 and
came to the United States in 1941. Although I have often gone
abroad, Chicago has been my permanent residence for four
decades. Thus, in two generations, my father and I have witnessed
well over a century of the most far-reaching and revolutionary
changes on both sides of the Pacific Ocean.

Life was quite unpredictable and enormously exciting to the
Japanese youths of my father's generation. After all, people in
Japan had had no contact with outsiders from 1641, when the
Tokugawa *shōgunate* imposed national seclusion, until 1854, when
Japan was reopened under pressure from Commodore Matthew
Perry. The architects of modern Japan under the Meiji Emperor
(r. 1867-1912) were pragmatic statesmen who wanted to utilize
Western learning and technology to strengthen their island empire.
In other parts of the world, Western colonial powers imposed
"Westernization," but in modern Japan leaders actively sought
things Western according to Japanese priorities as defined by the
government. The guiding principle of modern Japan was the Con-
fucian-based slogan, *Tōyō no dōtoku, Seiyō no gakugei* ("Eastern
ethics and Western science").[1] That is to say, they wanted to import only the practical learning and technologies which would help
strengthen the coherence and the authoritarian structure of
Japanese government, culture, and society. Nevertheless, once the
Japanese people, especially ambitious and iconoclastic youths, felt
emancipated from their nation's feudal past, they eagerly welcomed
not only the technologies but also the ideological components of
Western civilization, from philosophy, religion, and the social sciences to the education of women.[2] Ironically, it was the Neo-Confucian principle ("There is only one *li* ['reason' or 'truth'] in the
world") that encouraged youths like my father to espouse the
Christian religion, even though to a great extent they continued to
preserve the Confucian metaphysical intuition under Christian
symbolism.

The reopening of Japan enabled the Japanese to learn directly
what was happening in other parts of the world. Many people took
a keen interest in the opening of the Suez Canal, the unification of

Italy, the formation of the new Germany, and the establishment of the British Indian empire. Inevitably, knowledge of the West split the Japanese into two camps, pro-European and anti-European. Marius Jensen quotes the statement in 1887 of the pro-Western foreign minister, Inouye Kaoru: "Let us change our empire into a European-style empire. Let us change our people into European-style people. Let us create a new European-style empire on the Eastern sea."[3]

The anti-Western Japanese, however, were quick to point out the expansionist policies of Western nations, especially their encroachment into China following the Opium War.[4]

The brute force of the Western powers involved in international affairs was emulated by Japanese leaders who were building the nation on the principles of a strong economy and a strong defense system (*fukoku kyōhei*). Both of these made Japan a strange new imperial power in Asia, as exemplified by the Sino-Japanese War (1894-1895), the Russo-Japanese War (1904-1905), and the annexation of Korea (1910); and even the most pro-Western elements began to be influenced by the rising "New Japanism."[5]

The contents of this particular "New Japanism" indicated a strange fusion of "Chinese philology, Japanese loyalism, and Western science,"[6] but its focus had been on Japan itself. In fact, Japanese thought has always oscillated between "particularism" (e.g., various kinds of Japanism at different phases of Japanese history) and "universalism" (e.g., Confucianism and Buddhism). As I have often remarked, the curse and hallmark of Japanese culture and religion has been their propensity to subjugate universal principles, such as the Chinese *tao* and the Buddhist *dharma*, under the authority of the throne, authenticated by the particularistic Shinto myths or the authority of the *shōgun*, supported by the combination of a Shinto-Buddhist amalgam and indigenized Confucian tradition. The development of successive Japanisms, all quite eclectic in nature, presupposed the existence of the highest authority, that of either the emperor or the *shōgun*. Understandably, the late nineteenth century version of the "New Japanism" was warmly welcomed by the Meiji government, determined to develop an entirely new "super-religion" called "State Shinto" to which every Japanese subject, regardless of his or her religious affiliation, had to pay homage.

In retrospect, it becomes evident that the government during the Meiji, Taishō, and pre-war Shōwa eras successfully intimidated the leaders and institutions of Buddhism, Sect-Shinto denominations, Christianity, and others; but the government was less successful, and thus more cautious, in dealing with universities, especially the imperial universities. In the main, Japanese universities were modelled after Western institutions. Not only did the curricula of Japanese universities follow those of their European and American counterparts, but they also adopted Western, especially Greek, philosophies as the required subject matter of "philosophy" (*Tetsugaku*; note the absence of a modifier), whereas those who were interested in Chinese or Buddhist systems had to enroll in "Chinese philosophy" (*Chūgoku-tetsugaku*) or "Indian philosophy" (*Indo-tetsugaku*) respectively. It goes without saying that traditional philosophy in Japan had been invariably nurtured by Buddhist or Chinese patterns of thought; but modern Japanese philosophical systems, even those schools which reject Western solutions, have been greatly influenced by Western metaphysics—a possible explanation for both the fact that it is fairly easy for Western scholars to talk to Japanese philosophers, including Japanese Buddhist thinkers, and the fact that so many articulate Marxists have come out of Japanese universities. Thus, as Yoshinori Takeuchi says, the term philosophy refers to "the work of thinkers who have formulated their systems under the influence of Western philosophy." He continues: "Adopting Western methods, utilizing Western categories, and at the same time criticizing both, they endeavor to find a new way to express their original philosophical insights and often, in view of the results so far achieved, their own life and world views, nurtured in the tradition of Oriental thought."[7]

After the relatively liberal twenties, often called the period of Taishō democracy, the thirties ushered in an excessive form of

Japanism supported by jingoistic nationalism and aggressive militarism. All liberal thought and expression in philosophy (see above), religion, art, and culture were condemned as dangerous and un-Japanese. The rights of freedom of the press, thought, assembly, conscience, and belief were violated. Japanese armed forces invaded Manchuria and other parts of China. We liberal college students were dumbfounded by the attempted *coup d'etat* of the rightists in the so-called "2/26 affair" (February 26, 1936). All religious bodies—Buddhist, Christian, and Sect-Shinto denominations—were expected to cooperate with the national aim of extending imperial rule abroad. My aged father, thoroughly disgusted with the ultra-conservative government, died in 1939, worrying about the future of his beloved Japan. In 1940, Japan became a partner in the Rome-Berlin Tokyo axis. Early in 1941, I was able to leave Japan for the United States.

The dreadful news of Pearl Harbor was broadcast on a peaceful Sunday morning, December 7, 1941. Located in Berkeley, California, I was compelled to read about the feverish activities of many ultra-patriotic and/or anti-Oriental groups following the outbreak of war.[8] I was rounded up as an "enemy alien" early in 1942 along with some German and Italian aliens and transferred to the Department of Justice Detention Camp in Santa Fe, New Mexico. After a further stay in the Army Internment Camp in Lordsburg, New Mexico, I was shipped to Minidoka, the War Relocation Authority (Department of the Interior) center amidst the sagebrush in Hunt, Idaho, the camp for Americans of Japanese ancestry and their parents, who were considered aliens because of the law prohibiting Oriental immigrants from acquiring American citizenship. Thus I came to know intimately many *Isseis* (immigrants from Japan) and *Niseis* (the children of *Isseis*, who were American citizens by virtue of their birth in the United States).

This is not the place to write in detail about the wartime experiences of *Isseis* and *Niseis* in America. Briefly stated, shortly after the beginning of the war, West Coast pressure groups cried out not only for the evacuation of alien Japanese but also for the removal of all American citizens of Japanese descent. According to the curious logic of Earl Warren, then Attorney General of the State of California and later Chief Justice of the Supreme Court of the United States, the absence of sabotage in the early months of the war was a positive indication that Americans of Japanese ancestry were planning a dangerous and far-reaching program of concerted sabotage. The climax came in the spring of 1942, when the Commanding General of the Western Defense Command, John L. DeWitt, on the grounds of military necessity, ordered all persons of Japanese descent—most of them American citizens—to be removed from their homes on the West Coast to ten centers of concentration—like the Minidoka center—located in the remote interior of America. In his official recommendation for evacuation, DeWitt made this revealing statement: "The Japanese race is an enemy race, and while many second and third generation Japanese have become Americanized, the racial strains are undiluted."[9]

Thus 110,000 persons of Japanese descent—citizens and aliens alike—were evacuated from their homes with no official charge filed against them and with no evidence of guilty conduct attributed to them. This mass evacuation of persons of Japanese ancestry shocked many Americans concerned with civil rights. Mr. Justice Murphy stated: "Distinctions based on color and ancestry are utterly inconsistent with our traditions and ideas. They are at variance with the principles for which we are now waging war. . . . To say that any group cannot be assimilated is to admit that the great American experiment failed, that our way of life has failed when confronted with the normal attachment of certain groups to the lands of their forefathers."[10] That the evacuation of the Japanese Americans from the West Coast was the result of regional pressure groups becomes evident from the fact that a majority of persons of Japanese ancestry was allowed to remain in Hawaii throughout the war—an area located in the heart of the Pacific War.

When the war was over I felt called to work for Japanese-Americans who had moved to Chicago while at the same time continuing my work at the University of Chicago. I was persuaded that we either had to forget the sad experience of the mass evacuation or learn some lessons from it. The fact that the bulk of the population had never known the truth was problematic, and if people thought about it at all they were inclined to accept unthinkingly that "the government" probably knew best, without remembering that *they* were responsible for the government. Back then I once wrote:

> The scars remain. Personal resources have been wiped out. Parents' relationships with their children have been jeopardized. People have lost confidence in themselves and in American society. Youngsters have acquired manners and outlooks quite foreign to 'outside' standards. Surely this cannot happen again![11]

I worked for the smooth resettlement of Japanese-Americans in Chicago until 1951, supported by the Episcopal Church, opening up housing and securing jobs for *Isseis* and *Niseis* regardless of their religious backgrounds. I was moved by so many fair-minded Americans, especially those belonging to the "peace churches"—the Quakers and Brethren especially—who went out of their way to help members of minority groups. Even today I cherish the friendship I found among social workers, church leaders, educators, secular community organizers, and Jewish and Black colleagues.

It was not easy to lead two different lives, but I must admit that I enjoyed my graduate work in the history of religions enormously, partly because of the warm personality and impressive erudition of my mentor, Joachim Wach (1898-1955), scion of the family of Moses Mendelssohn and Felix Mendelssohn-Bartholdy. He taught us to respect the uniqueness of every religion and culture but to view each religious and cultural tradition from the perspective of the whole, i.e., through the religious experience of all of humankind, past, present, and future. Due to his "ethnic" background, Wach's teaching appointment at Leipzig had been terminated in 1935 through pressure from the Nazi regime. He thus had a special sympathetic understanding of the plight of Japanese-Americans during World War II. (I remember that he was particularly kind to Yoshiaki Fujitani, now Bishop of the Honpa Honganji Buddhist Mission in Honolulu.) Many of his interesting friends visited his classes, among them Martin Buber, D.T. Suzuki,

Gershom Scholem, G. van der Leeuw, Jacques Duchesne-Guillemin, A.A. Fyzee, Swami Akhilananda, Hideo Kishimoto, and Ernst Benz. That University of Chicago students had access to such world-renowned scholars was—and still is—a product of its policy to function primarily as a full-scale graduate institution and to eschew the system of teaching assistantships.

Chicago in the mid-forties was an exciting place. Its chancellor was Robert Maynard Hutchins, who had assumed the presidency before his thirtieth year. The university had a galaxy of inspiring, if controversial, figures on its faculty, including Rex Tugwell, Charles Merriam, Enrico Fermi, Paul Douglas, Robert Redfield, Richard McKeon, Charles Hartshorne, James Luther Adams, Amos Wilder, Ralph Marcus, and John Nef. It was indeed exhilarating to study here in those days. My wife, Evelyn, received her Ph.D. in 1950, although she had begun teaching in the Sociology department in 1948 or 1949. Wach recommended me to teach in the Divinity School in 1951 when I completed my degree; and I also joined the Committee of Far Eastern Civilizations which, to my amazement, taught Chinese but not Japanese. We soon rectified that situation. At this time, the university had departmental libraries scattered all over the campus. I spent a great deal of time chasing books from one to another. I marvelled at the curious imagination of librarians who, for example, placed the book entitled *The University of Nalanda*, involving primarily ancient Buddhist monastic life, in the Education Library.

Having accepted the teaching position, I still had more mundane problems to solve, problems which in those days presented a challenge. It was still so soon after the war, for example, that the American Automobile Association was not admitting to membership people with Japanese names. Thus for a time we had to drive without the benefit of protection. We also had our share of difficulties in purchasing a co-op apartment.

During these years the relationship between America and Japan steadily improved. Daily I received letters from Japan, some from old acquaintances but more from strangers who knew someone who had read something I had written and were now asking of me one or another kind of favor. I was surprised, too, at the number of visitors representing various departments of the government and educational and religious institutions who arrived in Chicago at odd times expecting to be met by someone who spoke both Japanese and English. We also had many students, war-brides, and other visitors who needed help.

In addition to mail and visitors, the improvement of America's relations with Japan brought me numerous invitations to speak at meetings, seminars, and conferences on aspects of Japan or Asia, past and present. I remember being surprised on being asked to represent the United States at one of the UNESCO or UN (I don't remember which) conferences in San Francisco. I gave, I think, four talks on Japan over the campus radio station for the university dormitories; and the university's radio program, "The Round Table," asked me to talk to notable figures from around the world, including the United States Ambassador to Israel and the former United States High Commissioner in Bavaria. I was literally tongue-tied on three occasions while talking with Arnold Toynbee, Bertrand Russell, and Sarvepalli Radhakrishnan.

In the summer of 1954, the Canadian Broadcasting Corporation asked me to help them cover the second assembly of the World Council of Churches (WCC), held at Northwestern University in Evanston, Illinois. The some thirteen hundred ecumenical leaders from various continents included many unforgettable people, especially those from behind the Iron Curtain. A year later, the WCC invited me to its conference in Davos, Switzerland. At the time, I was a man without a passport, since my Japanese student passport, issued before the war, could not be renewed during the war. Since I planned to remain permanently in Chicago, I decided to secure American citizenship, an endeavor in which I was greatly aided by the office of Paul Douglas, formerly a professor of economics at the University of Chicago and then a senator from Illinois. Thus I left for Europe with a brand-new American passport, first spending a week at Albert Schweitzer College before going on to the Davos conference. At its close, my wife and I travelled to Orselina-Locarno, where my mentor, Joachim Wach, was visiting his mother and sister. We were distressed and disappointed to find him quite ill, but with his physician's assurances of a sure recovery, we went on to other places in Europe. While in London, we received the sad news of his death; he was just fifty-eight.[12] We returned to Switzerland for the funeral to hear from his sister that Mircea Eliade, a renowned historian of religions, was attending the Eranos Conference in nearby Ascona. Although I went to Ascona to see him, he had left. I later wrote to him of Wach's death and asked him to consider coming to teach at the University of Chicago.

In the autumn of 1955, Wach's teacher, Friedrich Heiler, came to Chicago from Marburg. The next summer I attended another WCC conference in Herrenalb, Germany, after which I went again to Switzerland, this time to attend the funeral of Wach's mother. That year I did meet Eliade, who agreed to deliver the Haskell Lectures and to teach for one year at the University of Chicago. He had a Bollingen Foundation grant to write books and didn't need any more income; he and his wife had the use of the elegant apartment of a French physician friend in Paris, who had left for Port Said after being assigned to the Suez Canal Zone. To make a long story short, this friend had to return unexpectedly to Paris when Nasser nationalized the Suez, so the Eliades decided to stay in Chicago longer than just the one year. Actually, they stayed for three decades at the University of Chicago, until Eliade's death in 1986.[13]

In 1957, I was asked to organize the Paul Carus Memorial Symposium.[14] This was the first time that a group of important American historians of religions had met under one roof, and it was from this humble beginning that the American Society for the Study of Religion (ASSR) developed two years later. The Carus family was delighted to welcome the return of D.T. Suzuki, who had spent more than ten years with them at the turn of the century. We were also pleased to welcome a visiting professor and his wife from Japan, Professor and Mrs. Hori Ichiro. We, the Eliades and the Horis often shared dinner and conversation.

In 1958, a Rockefeller Foundation grant enabled my wife and I to take a one-year trip around the world.[15] We spent the summer at Mt. Kōya. The 9th Congress of the International Association for the History of Religions (IAHR) met that year for the first time outside of Europe in Tokyo and Kyoto. It was marvelous to see so many Japanese historians of religions and their counterparts from Europe and other continents.[16] Immediately after the official session, we went to see the puppet show (*Bunraku*) in Osaka, and then we and the Eliades and Joseph Campbell took an inland sea boat trip to Beppu, followed by a short visit to Unzen (a spa). Some of our hilarious escapades are recorded in Eliade's *No Souvenirs: Journal, 1957-1969*.[17] At the close of the conference, Joachim Wach's sister, Suzanne, visited us in Japan; she was well looked after by her brother's former students, e.g., Professor Hirai Naofusa of Kokugakuin University.

We left Japan for Hong Kong, Saigon, Angkor Wat (Cambodia), Singapore, and other Southeast and South Asian countries early in 1959; and everywhere we met politicians, diplomats, scholars, representatives of the Asia Foundation, and students.[18] I sensed in Saigon that the French cultural influence and the American military presence could not for long subdue a rising nationalism. The political situation in Indonesia prevented our visiting there. In Burma I had an "audience" (and I use this expression advisedly) with the deposed former Buddhist premier, U Nu. In Rangoon and Colombo and Bangkok I was greatly impressed by a new Asian phenomenon, namely, the fusion of religious, cultural, and political dynamics. Our visit to Madras, India, coincided with the arrivals of such notables as Prince Philip, Marshall Tito, and Martin Luther King. The fact that King was the greatest attraction of the three told us something. Although we were able to meet many people and to see religious establishments in India and Nepal, we could not get to Kashmir because of plane problems. We were, however, able to meet Dag Hammarskjold at the Aśoka Hotel on United Nations Day and wondered how in the climate of New Delhi it was possible for the stage for "Holiday on Ice" to be set up!

I took the opportunity to visit Israel and some of the Islamic nations, although not Syria and Iran where the political situation prevented entry. I was amused at being taken for an Indonesian at Al

Azhar (the Vatican of Islam) in Cairo. It is heartbreaking to think that Beirut, one of the world's most charming cities, has been ruined by incessant warfare. After seeing the Palestinian refugee camps, I was convinced that peace could never come to the Near East without an improvement in their miserable situation. This was 1959, and we had to carry our bags through the Mandelbaum Gate that divided the Muslim and Jewish sections of Jerusalem. We weren't prepared for the fifteen-minute time difference between the Islamic and Jewish sides! We were greatly impressed by the vitality of the new nation of Israel and awed by the erudition of Gershom Scholem, classmate of my mentor, Joachim Wach, and truly an embodiment of dedication to scholarship. Our journey to Israel became a pleasant and illuminating experience, thanks largely to the thoughtfulness of our hosts, R.J. Zwi Werblosky and his wife, Aliza.

Our time in Europe was very limited, but we managed to see famous places in Turkey, Greece, and Italy. We were impressed by the learning and personalities of Giuseppe Tucci and Raffaele Pettazzoni in Rome. After spending some time with my brother, Daisuke, and my friend, Harry B. Partin, in Geneva, I delivered the Wach Memorial Lecture at the Philipps-Universität in Marburg.[19]

In 1959, our book dedicated to the memory of Joachim Wach was published.[20] In 1960, we attended the 10th Congress of the IAHR in Marburg. It was a memorable occasion in so many ways. Friedrich Heiler greeted the participants in twenty or more languages. My presentation of "Emperor and Shaman" was inhibited by the attendance of Prince Takahito Mikasa of Japan, but I muddled through somehow. In 1961, the University of Chicago Press started the publication of our journal, *History of Religions*.

I spent 1961-62 in the Far East researching modern Chinese Buddhism, having received with my friend, Holmes H. Welch, a research grant from the Social Science Research Council. The highlight of our year was attending the conference of the World Fellowship of Buddhists in Phnom Penh, Cambodia late in 1961. We stayed in a hotel along with delegates from Russia, China, and Mongolia. As I recall, the Russians and the Chinese were still quite chummy in those days.[21] Early in 1962, I had a long personal interview with Dr. Hu Shih of Academica Sinica in Taipei only a few days before his death.[22] I also called on the Taoist Pope.

In 1962-63, I served as the American Council of Learned Societies' annual Lecturer on the History of Religions: I was asked to deliver five lectures on Japanese religion.[23] That my itinerary included many institutions from Harvard to Claremont was most profitable for me as far as finding jobs for our graduates and recruiting talented students for Chicago were concerned. In September, 1965, the 11th Congress of the IAHR was held, for the first time in North America, in Claremont, California.[24] At its close, I hurried back to Chicago in order to prepare for a conference on the history of religions to be held as part of the celebration of the seventy-fifth anniversary of the founding of the University of Chicago. After the final presentation, a public lecture by Paul Tillich, several people—including the Tillichs and the Eliades—came over to our home for relaxed conversation. That night Paul Tillich was taken to the hospital where he died a few days later.[25]

Paul Tillich had been teaching every winter at the University of California at Santa Barbara, and his salary had been budgeted for his stay at the time of his death. The university attempted to persuade Eliade to take his place for the winter, but Eliade was busy with his current novel and declined; so I spent the winter of 1966 teaching at Santa Barbara. In 1967, we celebrated the sixtieth birthday of Mircea Eliade.[26] In the spring of 1968, I was honored to serve as the Charles Wesley Brashares Lecturer on the History of Religions at Northwestern University in Evanston, Illinois. I also served as a resource person for the China seminar on "After Mao and Ching," sponsored by the Council on Religion and International Affairs, held at Solvang, California.[27] That summer the Faculty Seminar on Buddhism, sponsored jointly by the Associated Colleges of the Midwest and the Great Lakes Association, asked me to direct the program at Carleton College in Northfield, Minnesota. Although Edward Conze, whom we had invited, could not enter the United States because of technicalities with Immigration, Walpola Rahula of Sri Lanka was able to come and enlighten

seminar participants. I was also happy that our cooperative translation project for Asian religious texts was successfully completed
that year.[28]   Meanwhile I was persuaded to chair the Agenda
Committee, whose task was to pinpoint issues for the faculty discussions that would determine the future of the Divinity School;
and I was elected to a three-year term as president of the American
Society for the Study of Religion.

   The year 1970 was an eventful year. My brother, Daisuke, died
in Switzerland in the spring. In July, I assumed the Deanship of
the Divinity School with Martin E. Marty as my Associate Dean; I
stayed on in that capacity until 1980. In August, the 12th Congress
of the IAHR was held in Stockholm, Sweden, and I served on its
International Committee and the Advisory Board of its official or-
gan, *NVMEN*. At home, representatives of university-based divinity schools, including Harvard, Yale, Vanderbilt, and Chicago, had
their first meeting in Chicago; they subsequently met from time to
time for mutual edification and fund-raising. In 1972 James M.
Gustafson, then at Yale, returned to Chicago as University Professor. In the summer of 1973, I participated in the regional IAHR
Study Conference on Methodology, held in Turku, Finland.[29] In
the autumn of 1974, the Divinity School, in cooperation with the
Jesuit School of Theology and the Catholic Theological Union,
sponsored a month-long "Celebration of the Medieval Heritage,"
inviting Helder Camara, Archbishop of Olinda and Recife, Brazil;
Franziskus Koenig, Cardinal Archbishop of Salzburg; Bernard
Lonergan, S.J.; Karl Rahner, S.J.; and Sargent Shriver, among oth-
ers. In December, 1974, the Divinity School hosted the ceremony
at which Reinhold Niebuhr Awards were presented to Andrei
Sakharov, a Soviet scientist (the award was received for him by
Pavel Litvinov) and Pastor C.F. Beyers Naude of South Africa.
The occasion brought to our campus Mrs. R. Niebuhr, Roger
Baldwin, Hans Morganthau, Arthur M. Schlessinger, Rose Styron,
and Robert McAfee Brown. In 1975, I was able to persuade Anne
Carr, the first woman to serve on our faculty, to return to her alma
mater as Assistant Dean.

In the summer of 1975 I spent a week in New Zealand and then visited major universities in Australia as the Charles Strong Memorial Lecturer.[30] I could not attend the 13th Congress of the IAHR held that year in Lancaster, England, although I was notified later that I was to serve as the organization's vice-president, an office I held until 1985. In 1976 my turn came to serve as the chairman of the History of Religions Committee of the American Council of Learned Societies, a duty from which I was relieved in 1985, and to serve as the vice-president of the UNESCO-based Conseil International de la Philosophie et des Sciences Humaines until 1982. In 1977, the Divinity School and the Union of American Hebrew Congregations co-sponsored a conference on the Jewish religious tradition entitled "Worship and Transcendence"; I spent that summer teaching at the University of Tokyo as a Japan Society for the Promotion of Science (JSPS) Visiting Professor; in 1977 we held a conference on "Religious Studies and Humanities: Theories of Interpretation," at which participants included Paul Ricoeur, Hans-Georg Gadamer, Mircea Eliade, Theodore Ziolkowski, Eugene Eoyang, Matei Calinescu, and Anthony C. Yu, among others.

In 1978, Hanna H. Gray was inaugurated as the tenth President of the University of Chicago. I was able to process the appointments of Hans Dieter Betz (New Testament), Wendy D. O'Flaherty (Indic Studies and the History of Religions), Robin W. Lovin (Ethics and Society), Samuel Sandmel (Helen A. Regenstein Professor of Religion), and of Stephen Toulmin of Social Thought and Fazlur Rahman of Islamics as associate members of the Divinity School. In 1979, the Divinity School dedicated the John Nuveen Wing, which houses the Institute for the Advanced Study of Religion, an arm of the Divinity School which attracts scholars from various parts of North America and abroad. In July of that year, I returned to Marburg for the sad duty of delivering a memorial lecture for my esteemed friend, Ernst Benz; and in September I visited Eastern Europe in connection with the IAHR regional study conference held in Warsaw Poland.[31] It was fortunate that Franklin I. Gamwell and James W. Lewis were added to the faculty of the Divinity School in Autumn, 1979, for in 1980 I stepped down from the deanship, succeeded by Mr. Gamwell (Mr. Lewis became the Dean of Students).

In the summer of 1980, I attended the 14th Congress of the IAHR, held in Winnipeg, Canada.[32] Since 1980, I have directed my share of doctoral dissertations, have taught the expected courses, and have served on a number of committees both in the Divinity School and in the Department of Far Eastern Languages and Civilizations, chairing such university-wide committees as the Committee to Eliminate Weak Academic Programs and the Committee for Honorary Degrees. I also accepted several short-term visiting professorships at such institutions as the Pacific School of Religion, Mills College, the University of Tennessee, the University of Iowa, and Princeton University.

In September of 1981, I was invited by the Chinese Academy of Science to visit China as a member of the University of Chicago delegation.[33] I was privileged to lecture at the University of Peking and to confer with many Chinese scholars of religions.

In 1983, we had a conference on the methodology of the history of religions with presentations by Mircea Eliade and Paul Ricoeur of the University of Chicago, Michael Meslin of the Sorbonne, Ninian Smart of the Universities of Lancaster and California at Santa Barbara, and Charles H. Long of the University of North Carolina.[34]

In addition, my religious/social/political activities and close work with like-minded people in Jewish, Catholic, and Protestant groups led to my serving as rapporteur at a conference on United States refugee policy held in Washington, D.C. in 1983.[35] Late that spring I delivered the Channing Moore Williams Memorial Lecture at Rikkyo University and lectured elsewhere in Japan.[36] My non-academic activities included membership on the board of the Robert Maynard Hutchins Center for the Study of Democratic Institutions in Santa Barbara; the board of the Woodstock Theological Center at Georgetown University, Washington, D.C.; the Council of Scholars of the Library of Congress, Washington, D.C.; and the Editorial Board of the Scholars Press in Atlanta, Georgia.

My university honored me greatly with the invitation to give the eleventh John Nuveen Lecture in 1983.[37]

A prolonged abdominal illness, requiring three major operations in the autumn of 1984, changed all my plans. I officially retired from the faculty of the University of Chicago in the spring of 1985.[38] With the help of friends, however, I was able to attend the 15th Congress of the IAHR in Sydney, Australia, in the summer of 1985, and the conference on post-war Japan at Rikkyo University the following December. Otherwise, my daily activities have mostly consisted of following the routine of exercises as prescribed by my physician and working on the sixteen-volume *Encyclopaedia of Religion*, issued from the Macmillan Publishing Company in 1987. Most lamentably, its Editor-in-Chief, Mircea Eliade, passed away in April 1986.

* * * * *

As I look back over my life—my childhood and youth in Japan and forty-five years outside the land of my birth—I certainly have no regrets. Life in the United States has been a most satisfying and rewarding experience, for unlike many parts of Europe and Asia, where people treat you as forever an outsider, in America one is expected to do one's share for the common good. In spite of some obvious unpleasantness and racial discrimination, one discovers in the United States that he or she is basically regarded as an individual.

Over the years I have come to realize that there are two types of people, specialists and generalists. I am not, by temperament or training, a specialist. I have my share of natural attachment to my culture, religion, and country; but I have come to appreciate the value and importance of the total experience of humankind. I am sure that there will always be a variety of religions, cultures, and nationalities. Do we sing the same song with different tunes? Or do we sing different songs with similar tunes? It seems to me that the reality of life, including the life of religion, is full of mystery; it is beyond our cognitive efforts, capacities, and achievements. I have met a number of truly bilingual persons, and I feel that similar talents, sensitivities, and training will be called for in the domains of both culture and religion. No wonder people are beginning to take seriously such expressions as "anonymous Buddhist" and "anonymous Christian." After living in different parts of the world, I now have great respect for patriotism but little use for nationalism. Certainly one loves one's country, despite its shortcomings; but one should not use his or her own nation as a yardstick to measure other nations. Similar principles should be operating as well in the domain of language, religion, and culture. More importantly, I have learned from various religions the simple truth that life is a pilgrimage through this mysterious universe. The homeless exile in our time portrays the experience of humanity more genuinely than do our fond dreams of a routine and fixed, settled life.

We are told that it was Benjamin Franklin's pious hope that love of liberty would permeate all corners of the earth, so that people could settle anywhere and say, "This is my Country."[39] I seriously doubt whether the world will be so altered any time soon. Nevertheless, some of us have already experienced bilingual or bicultural life and feel quite at home living on either side of the ocean. Certainly, even during my own lifetime we have moved far beyond the old, stereotyped notions of East and West. It may well be that today we are standing at the edge of a new era, and that all the upheavals and contradictions around us may be signs of our passing into a different and beneficial future. Let us hope and pray that it is so.

Notes

1 See Ryūsaku Tsunoda *et al.*, compilers, *Sources of Japanese Tradition* (New York: Columbia University Press, 1958), 607.

2 See Inazō Nitobe *et al.*, *Western Influences in Modern Japan* (Chicago: University of Chicago Press, 1931).

3 Marius Jensen, *Japan and Its World* (Princeton: Princeton University Press, 1980), 69.

4 See K.M. Panikkar, *Asia and Western Dominance* (London: G. Allen and Unwin, 1953), 259-70.

5 Jensen, 68ff.

6 Jensen, 71.

7 Yoshinori Takeuchi, "Modern Japanese Philosophy," *Encyclopaedia Britannica*, XVII, 1966 ed., 958J-959.

8 See Morton Grodzins, *Americans Betrayed: Politics and the Japanese Evacuation* (Chicago: University of Chicago Press, 1949), 19-61.

9 See Jacobus ten Broek *et al.*, *Prejudice, War, and the Constitution. Causes and Consequences of the Evacuation of the Japanese Americans in World War II* (Berkeley: University of California Press, 1954), 263.

10 Milton R. Konvitz, *The Alien and the Asiatic in American Law* (Ithaca: Cornell University Press, 1946), 248-49.

11 J.M. Kitagawa, "This Cannot Happen Again!" *Living Church*, CXI (November 1945), 11.

12 See my introduction, "The Life and Thought of Joachim Wach," in his posthumous publication, *The Comparative Study of Religions*, ed. by Joseph M. Kitagawa (New York: Columbia University Press, 1958); and J.M. Kita-

gawa, ed., *Understanding and Believing: Essays by Joachim Wach* (New York: Harper and Bros., 1968).

13 Probably the best single book on Eliade's life and thought is his *Ordeal by Labyrinth: Conversations with Claude-Henri Rocquet*, trans. by D. Coltmann (Chicago: University of Chicago Press, 1982).

14 See *Modern Trends in World Religions*, ed. by J.M. Kitagawa (LaSalle: The Open Court Press, 1959).

15 See my *Religions of the East* (Philadelphia: The Westminster Press, 1968).

16 See J.M. Kitagawa, "Sanka-gaijin-gakusha no yokogao," *Gakujutsu Geppo* (Japanese Scientific Monthly), XI (October 1958), 448-52.

17 Mircea Eliade, *No Souvenirs: Journal, 1957-1969*, trans. by F.H. Johnson, Jr. (New York: Harper and Row, 1977).

18 See my "Search for Self-Identity: Asian Peoples Today," *Divinity School News* XXVI (November 1959), 10-32.

19 See J.M. Kitagawa, *Gibt es ein Verstehen Fremder Religionen?* (Leiden: E.J. Brill, 1963).

20 See M. Eliade and J.M. Kitagawa, eds., *The History of Religions: Essays in Methodology* (Chicago: University of Chicago Press, 1959).

21 See my "Asia Revisited," *Criterion*, (Summer 1962), 31-35.

22 See my article, "Koteki Hakase," *Tokyo Mainichi* (March 1962).

23 See my *Religion in Japanese History* (New York: Columbia University Press, 1966).

24 See my contribution, "Gohei Hasami: A Rite of Purification of Time at Mt. Kōya," *Proceedings of the 9th Congress of the International Association for the History of Religions* Vol. II *Guilt or Pollution and Rites of Purification* (Leiden: E.J. Brill, 1968).

25 See J.M. Kitagawa, ed., *The History of Religions: Essays on the Problem of Understanding* (Chicago: University of Chicago Press, 1967).

26 See J.M. Kitagawa and C.H. Long, eds., *Myths and Symbols: Studies in Honor of Mircea Eliade* (Chicago: University of Chicago Press, 1969).

27 See J.M. Kitagawa, ed., *Understanding Modern China* (Chicago: Quadrangle Books, 1969).

28 See Wing-tsit Chan, Isma'il R. al Fārūqī, J.M. Kitagawa, and P.T. Raju, *The Great Asian Religions: An Anthology* (New York: Macmillan, 1969).

29 My contribution, "Early Shinto: A Case Study (Literary Source Criticism)," was later published in L. Honko, ed., *Science of Religion: Studies in Methodology* (The Hague: Mouton, 1979).

30 See my article, "Reality and Illusion: Some Characteristics of the Early Japanese 'World of Meaning,' " *Journal of the Oriental Society of Australia*, II (1976).

31 See my article, "Random Reflections on Methodological Problems of the History of Religions," in W. Tyloch, ed., *Current Progress in the Methodology of the Science of Religions* (Warsaw: Polish Scientific Publishers, 1984).

32 See my article, "Humanistic and Theological History of Religions," *NUMEN* XXVII, (December 1980), 198-219.

33 See my article, "Glimpse of China," *Criterion* XXI (Spring 1982).

34 See J.M. Kitagawa, ed., *The History of Religions: Retrospect and Prospect* (New York: Macmillan, 1985).

35 See J.M. Kitagawa, ed., *American Refugee Policy: Some Ethical and Religious Reflections* (Minneapolis: Winston Press, 1984).

36 See my Japanese book, *Gendai-sekai to Shūkyō-gaku* (Shinkyo Shuppansha, 1985).

37 See my booklet, *The 1893 World's Parliament of Religions and Its Legacy* (Chicago: The Divinity School, 1984).

38 See *Criterion*, XXIV (Autumn 1985).

39 Told by S.E. Mead in his article, "Christendom, Enlightenment, and the Revolution," in J.C. Brauer, ed., *Religion and American Revolution* (Philadelphia: Fortress Press, 1976), 50.

Chapter One

The Eastern "World of Meaning"

East and West

One of the paramount concerns of our time is the relationship between the East and the West. The frequent use of the expression "East and West" in daily conversation, in the media, and in the titles of articles and popular books seems to indicate the extent to which people of diverse backgrounds have become concerned with this topic. The expression "East and West," like other catchy phrases, has many different meanings, but by and large it refers to the two great cultural traditions found on either side of the Eurasian continent—Asia on the one hand and Europe (often including North America) on the other.

It is an irony and a great tragedy that our preoccupation with the East-West relationship has not resulted in closer and deeper understanding between the two cultures. Northrop, it is true, is said to have dispelled the persistent myth that East and West would never meet—a myth ascribed to the false prophecy of Rudyard Kipling. But "meeting" implies more than two parties facing each other with mutual ignorance and deep-rooted suspicion, and "understanding" does not mean judging the other side by one's own parochial standards. In this respect, both the Easterner and the Westerner have a long way to go before they learn to engage in effective dialogue. If I were addressing an Eastern audience, I would criticize some Easterners' one-sided and myopic views of the Western and our global situation. However, since I am now addressing myself to the Westerner, I will endeavor to present the Eastern situation as best I can, and will point out some things that might improve the East-West dialogue.

Having been in the United States for over four and a half decades, I should be used to the average American's indifference to other peoples, languages, religions, and cultures, but I am still shocked by it. For instance, in 1942, according to Harold Isaacs, more than 40 percent of the American population could not locate China or India on a map. In 1945, after America's military involvement on the Pacific front during World War II, only 43 and 45 percent of Americans could locate China and India, respectively.[1] I am also distressed by the confusion on the part of an amazing number of Americans who equate the domestic situation of Americans of Oriental ancestry and the world-wide phenomenon of intercultural relations.[2] Even on college and university campuses, where people presumably should know better, Americans of Asian descent are frequently invited to social events which are designed to welcome foreign students—not as hosts but as guests. Some of the churches of Asian Americans on the West Coast have been supported and administered by their respective denominations' departments of "foreign missions" as though Asian Americans were foreigners.

Today our ignorance of Eastern cultures and our confusing the American domestic problem involving peoples of Asian ancestry with the global phenomenon of inter-cultural relations are no longer tolerated as innocent and amusing matters because of a new factor, namely the profound and widespread impact of the East on the West. Shortly after the end of World War II, the learned Catholic scholar Henri de Lubac pointed out that Europe was ripe for spiritual colonization by the East.[3] This observation was shared by a leading Dutch Protestant scholar, Hendrik Kraemer, who also detected a spontaneous openness, a readiness to be invaded by the Orient, both in Europe and North America.[4] The impact of the East on the West today is multi-dimensional and far-reaching, involving the pictorial arts, novels, movies, flower arrangement, arts of self-defense, electronics, automobiles, various forms of meditation, a variety of new and old religious cults, an increasing number of Asian scientists and scholars in Western academic institutions, and a growing influx of Asian capital into the American economy.

We have reason to be comforted by the fact that our sensitivity to the East has been slowly improving, at least in some quarters, although it should make us uneasy to know that it took a major war to make East-West relations an issue. World War II marked a decisive turning point in the development of Asian studies in American colleges and universities. Before the war, American education, which was almost completely devoted to the study of the Western cultural tradition, produced educated citizens who knew practically nothing about the non-Western world. As Meribeth Cameron once quipped, "few Americans could name any Asiatics except Confucius, Gandhi and Chiang Kai-shek." But with the outbreak of hostilities, the national emergency required training programs in Asian subjects, and there appeared an amazing array of books and articles on Asia, from the very scholarly to the ridiculous. "Over night the few experts on the Far East who had been clinging to the fringes of American academic life became national assets. Audiences were eager to hear about Asia, conferences of specialist and laymen multiplied, and the academic world was edified by the spectacle of college administrators eager to inaugurate courses on the Far East at the very moment at which many of those best qualified to give them were being called into the armed forces or into government employment."[5] Happily, the newly aroused interest in Asia has been sustained to a remarkable degree in North American educational institutions since the end of World War II, although in recent years the focus has shifted from social scientific and humanistic aspects of Asia to the business and technological dimensions.

Of course, some educators and intellectuals have criticized, with some justification, hastily improvised courses on Asian subjects and have lamented the practice of devoting more time to the study of non-Western civilizations. For example, in 1951 Robert Maynard Hutchins, in his Preface to the *Great Books* series, gave fair warning: "The pretense that we are now prepared within the educational system to include understanding the East as one main pivot in a liberal curriculum will obstruct, not assist, the solution of the central problem of producing a liberally educated generation." While acknowledging the eventual necessity of learning about non-Western cultural traditions, Hutchins nevertheless asserted: "at the moment we have all we can do to understand ourselves in order to be prepared for the forthcoming meeting between East and West. . . . The time for that will come when we have understood our own tradition well enough to understand another."[6]

Undoubtedly there is some truth in Hutchins's assertion that an educated citizen must acquire skill in analysis, order in valuing, knowledge of history, and certain types of social experience so as to have a basis for judging and appreciating any cultural tradition, one's own or another's. But I seriously doubt that these skills in themselves are sufficient to enable one to deal with other cultural traditions. Also, I am not convinced that the time will ever come, as Hutchins seemed confident it would, "when we have understood our own tradition well enough to understand another." It is interesting to note that in the same volume Hutchins himself uses a different logic in connection with disarmament. According to him, "there are those who oppose the discussion of universal disarmament on the ground that disarmament is an effect and not a cause. They say that, until the tensions in the world are removed, disarmament cannot take place and that we shall simply deceive ourselves if we talked about it instead of doing something about the tensions." On this issue, Hutchins seems to be persuaded that one way to do something about the tensions is to talk about disarmament. Thus, "to refuse to discuss the principal method of mitigating tensions on the ground that they have to be mitigated before it is discussed does not seem to be the best way to mitigate them."[7] I only wish Hutchins had applied this argument to the East-West encounter.

Unfortunately, there are no short-cuts or easy solutions. We must with insight and perseverance try to develop a new outlook on the Eastern cultural tradition which views life and the world very differently from its Western counterpart, for it has been nurtured by different languages, values, historical experiences, and styles of life. We must also acknowledge that understanding the

Eastern cultural tradition is partly an effort to anticipate the kind
of world that is emerging before us, a world in which East and West
are destined to live together, influencing one another as partners
and sharing insights and resources. All this is, of course, easier said
than done. And we should not fall into the common error of as-
suming that pious pronouncements will automatically bring about a
better world.

Western Understanding of the East

Anyone who has crossed linguistic or cultural barriers can testify
to how difficult it is to carry on meaningful conversation across
these lines. On the most elementary level our natural tendency is
to see in others pretty much what we want and expect to see. Thus,
it is quite common for Western economists to be interested in the
economic aspect of Asia and for Asian artists to be fascinated by
Western art. Our mother tongues alone provide us with built-in
yardsticks for evaluating everything with which we come in contact,
so that some of what we know has to be unlearned.

There is much truth in the observation of William S. Haas who
compares the impulse toward "unity" in the Western tradition with
the acceptance of "juxtaposition" in the Eastern tradition. According to him, the inner continuity of Western civilization—its matrix, coherence and congruity—goes back to the Greeks who had
created their own world by integrating foreign elements as stimu-
lants for the creation of new cultural forms. "Then the Greek
spark sprang over to cognate Rome. Henceforth, this classic culture shaped the body of medieval civilization, Rome giving to the
Church its visible organization and Greek philosophical thought
permeating the structure of its dogma. Europe, thus integrated by
westernized Christianity, at last proceeded to the scientific and
technical stage, which was based on the secularization of the medieval world conception. . . ."[8] Thus, from the standpoint of Western civilization various new experiences, e.g. the Renaissance, Reformation, Counter-Reformation, the Enlightenment, etc. were to
be seen as parts of the great movement toward unity. This percep-

tion is strongly validated and endorsed by the notion of evolutionary time in Western civilization, for as Haas astutely points out, "time" in the West "is not an indifferent medium in which events occur chronologically as things exist simultaneously in space."[9] It is very tempting for many Westerners to accept the inevitable fate of the Westernization of the non-Western world on the grounds that colonialism, Christian world mission, *Pax Britannica*, etc. were visible signs of the expansion of Western civilization moving toward unity and thus to succumb to the temptation of writing off the entire Eastern tradition because of our belief in the inexorable march of time.

In sharp contrast to the Western motif of "unity," the Eastern traditions affirm the "juxtaposition" and co-existence of relative and autonomous cultural and religious systems, each regarded as authentic and legitimate in its own right. Admittedly, there are many samenesses and similarities between different cultural traditions, for peoples' biological cycles are similar—birth, adolescence, youth, adulthood, old age and death. People go through similar processes of socialization in homes, playgrounds and places of work. They get married, and children arrive. Invariably, people are confronted by the loss of loved ones and so experience how deeply grief touches the depths of our being. Such are the common human experiences which are constant for different cultures and religions. But obviously the ways of structuring these same experiences are not universally the same. For example, Indian and Chinese civilizations might look very similar from a distance, but upon close examination they have very little in common, with the exception of the historical Buddhist expansion from India to China.

Let us consider a little further the historical transmission of Buddhism. Spengler and others have seriously questioned how many of the main tenets of Buddhism were authentically understood by Chinese Buddhists. In Spengler's own words: "Even though Indians and Chinese in those days both felt as Buddhists, they were spiritually as far apart as ever. The same words, the same rites, the same symbols—but two different souls, each going its own way."[10] Although many Westerners who stand convinced of the inevitable movement toward unity may think Spengler's view too extreme, his logic may be very useful in articulating the pattern of "juxtaposition." We might also point out that even the satellite cultures of India or of China maintained relative autonomy and insularity in the past. There was little feeling on the part of each cultural tradition in Asia, large or small, that it belonged to a greater unified entity which might be termed an Eastern or Oriental culture, in spite of F.S.C. Northrop's famous theory of "the unity of Oriental culture."[11]

We should also point out that it is a common Western convention to divide human experience into such pigeon-holes as religion, culture, art, morality, commerce, politics, etc. This convention has been so deeply rooted in the Western tradition that many people think of it not only as pan-Western but also as universal. Once Paul Tillich told us of his sobering experience in talking to a Buddhist scholar in Kyoto. Evidently, the scholar asked Tillich why he assumed that the primordial character of reality is "being" and not "non-being," and Tillich confessed that it was his oversight not to examine the provincial Western premise of "being" as the basic category in talking to non-Western traditions. As Tillich's example dramatically exhibits, many Westerners who encounter Easterners often consider what has happened in the East during the past four centuries or so primarily as an appendage to the expansion of the West in its movement toward global unity. They also assume that reasonable Easterners would, or should, accept the Western convention of demarcating human experience as the only valid universal framework to be shared by Eastern and Western traditions.

Conversely, in encountering the Western tradition many Easterners—now that most of them have been emancipated from the yoke of Western colonialism—are inclined to think of the Western tradition as one of several equally legitimate and autonomous civilizations but having no claim to special status. Unfortunately, casual Western observers of the East can overlook the Eastern reality which is lying immediately under the modernized surface. It is so easy, for example, for Hilton-hopping tourists to get the impression that the non-Western world is becoming very westernized, based on the appearance of airports, skyscrapers, and shopping centers. Even more sophisticated businessmen and government officials, partly to overcompensate for their unfamiliarity with foreign languages and customs, often stick to the westernized image of the East. As Mircea Eliade used to say, many Westerners are not prepared emotionally to encounter the "strangeness" of other peoples and cultures, for they tend to depend on the more westernized representatives of Eastern peoples or enter into relations with the East only in such external spheres as economics and politics. Thus, in his own words: "The Western world has not yet, or not generally, met with authentic representatives of the 'real' non-Western traditions."[12]

There is much truth in Betty Heimann's observation that the profound gulf between the East and West is epitomized by the simple word "system" (*systema*), which literally connotes putting together, or putting in order. The underlying assumption here is that the "human mind thinks 'systematically,' prescribing the order of research, the selection, disposition and composition of ideas," whereas the Eastern mind is more intuitive and reflective. It is more likely "to look, to contemplate, to be receptive—but in no degree implying any idea of regulating the facts of nature."[13]

Similarly Lily Abegg, author of *Ostasien denkt anders* (translated somewhat blandly as *The Mind of East Asia*)[14] is of the opinion that the Western mind is more extroverted while the Asian mind is more introverted, with the result that the former is better equipped to understand the world of nature while the latter is better suited to understand the nature of the human being. Echoing Betty Heimann, Abegg too thinks that Westerners tend to grasp the nature of an object "objectively" and "analytically," whereas Asians tend to be more concerned with the act of "knowing" itself, which to them is an aspect of being. This may account for the frustration of many Westerners as they encounter Asians for the first time; Asians seem to talk in a circle without making direct statements about any subject matter. Many Asians, on the other hand, feel that Westerners are overly opinionated, making hasty judgments based on insufficient grounds. In the main, Asians approach an object in the same way an airplane circles several times before approaching an airport, even though they may not appear to be making an advance in any direction. "These advances," says Abegg, "are a mixture, psychically considered—partly intellectual, partly emotional, based partly on the senses and partly on the will."[15] And they do not arrive at a decision until they are in a state of total readiness; this fact often aggravates Westerners at international conferences.

It goes without saying that the mental attitude of Easterners has been nurtured by the tradition of "juxtaposition" of various cultural and religious collectivistic systems, each grounded in an eternal, cosmic principle. Such systems, which require as much conformity as efficiency, appear to Westerners as stifling. Thus, Western democratic crusaders are apt to preach to Asians the gospel of individualism, liberty and freedom as social, cultural, religious and political ideals. They wonder how peoples in various parts of Asia can live under authoritarian regimes. We might remember, on the other hand, that in Asia liberty has historically often connoted something licentious and uncontrolled. Many people associated liberty "with the wild animals of the jungle, or with primitive and barbaric tribes of nomads or hunters."[16] To many Asians, the accumulation of personal virtues and cultural values that can be transmitted from one generation to the next is more important and meaningful. The question is not which values—Eastern or Western—are more correct. Both have legitimate concerns which can be understood within the same cultural traditions but cannot be easily and immediately transferred to the other side. For instance, Yu-Kuang Chu rightly points out that the Western concept of the law of identity is determined by a language which has a subject and a predicate, whereas the Chinese, who do not depend on a subject of a verb, developed correlational logic. "The categories of Western thought are substance, causality, and identity. The Chinese are interested not in the nature of Heaven but the Will of Heaven as revealed in socio-political life. . . . The categories of Chinese thinking are correlational logic, analogical thought, and relational thinking, which though inappropriate to science are very useful in political theory.[17]

The foregoing makes it abundantly clear that the usual Western mode of thinking and the Western way of demarcating human experience are not the most reliable tools for understanding Asia. That is to say, in order to understand Eastern people, their cultural and religious traditions, we must enter as much as possible into the very structure of their languages, thoughts and spiritual experiences, and this takes more than sheer intellectual endeavor. In short, our effort to "understand" the East involves a more complete understanding, implying a sort of *metanoia*.

Since we are compelled to talk in generalities in order to save time and space, we might profitably focus discussion on three major points, namely, (i) the historical Asian "world of meaning" (which I intend to develop in this chapter), (ii) the impact of the West during the past four centuries or so, and (iii) the current state of affairs.

The Historical World of Meaning in Asia

In dealing with any cultural tradition, there are many approaches and a variety of perspectives, all of which are important. For example, one might profitably study works of art, architecture, music, philosophy, literature, religious, and legal institutions (realizing of course that these are very "Western" ways of dividing life that may not be entirely applicable to the Eastern situation), all of which provide some clues to our understanding of the ethos and character of a cultural tradition. I have opted in this book for an attempt to understand the "world of meaning," based on the simple premise that each individual, each culture, and each religion exists not only in a physical, geographical world, but also in the nebulous but seamless framework, coherence or matrix, which might be termed a "world of meaning." In many ways, this kind of "world of meaning" represents a life more real than the visible, physical world. After all, as William Earle rightly points out, culture "is a product of the human spirit, and that particular sort of product which is never finally produced; that is, culture is nothing but a *life* of human beings, and for culture to be alive means that actual human beings live in it."[18] Every culture provides a coherent "world of meaning" to those who live in that cultural tradition. For the most part, we inherit that which is handed down to us, e.g., languages, ideas, values and the small intimate habits of daily life.

Usually, our own self-image or self-identity is nurtured and sustained by our world of meaning. In this Asians are no exception. For example, in historical India many people found their self-identity through the institution called the *Varṇāśrama-dharma* system, which literally means "*dharma*" ("that which is established," duty or law) according to "*varṇa*" ("class" referring to one's given class, which exemplifies one's own development within the cycle of transmigration covering many lives) and "*āśrama*" ("stage of life," referring to one's given stage within one's own lifetime). Strange as it may seem to the Western mind, people in ancient India accepted as reasonable the physical and mental inequality of human beings at birth as the result of one's action in previous incarnations, resulting in one being born into the castes of *Brahmins* (priests), *Kṣatriyas* (warriors and rulers), *Vaiśyas* (merchants and husbandmen), or *Śūdras* (laborers and servants). Although individuals were considered responsible for their past actions, they anticipated rebirth into higher castes in future incarnations by faithfully discharging the duties of their given situations.

Nikhilānanda reminds us that "the four castes are the four principal parts of society, and therefore, their welfare depends upon the welfare of each. [Accordingly], a higher caste must show gentleness and compassion to a lower caste."[19] He also tells us that the term *āśrama* is derived from the root *śrama* ("to toil"), implying that "each stage in life and position in society has its appropriate duty, the right performance of which requires self-control and austerity."[20] The first stage of usually twelve years is that of the celibate student. Often students live in their teachers' houses, studying the sacred scriptures called the *Vedas*. The second stage is that of the householder, wherein the aspirant marries and discharges family and societal duties. During the third stage of the cycle, that of

the recluse, one relinquishes his family duties and retires into soli-
tude for contemplation. During the fourth and final stage, the
phase of the renouncer (*Sannyāsin*), one forsakes his caste and society entirely and devotes his life to cultivating the virtues of
chastity, poverty, truthfulness and abstinence. As such, the four
stages signify the process of one's progressive renunciation of
earthly attachment. "Every stage has its corresponding duties and
responsibilities. It is the duty of the student to acquire knowledge,
the duty of the householder to serve society according to his capa-
bility, the duty of the recluse to lead a life of contemplation, and
the duty of the *sannyāsin* to lead a life of purity, freedom, and
fearlessness. . . . He no longer strives for ethical perfection; virtue
embellishes all his actions. He devotes himself to the welfare of
others without seeking any personal gain."[21] Such was the ideal
norm of ancient Hindus' sense of self-identity.

It is interesting to note that there was another principle of self-
identity, emerging out of Indian soil, advocated by Buddha Gau-
tama, also known as Śākyamuni. Because shortly after the Buddha's
death Buddhists appropriated Brahmanic-Hindu modes of thinking
to explain Buddhist experience—not unlike the Hellenistic Jews
just prior to the beginning of the common era who appropriated
Greek thought to elucidate Hebrew religiosity—many Hindus, and
some Buddhists, think of Buddhism, erroneously, as an offshoot of
Brahmanic-Hinduism. And, as much as many of the Hellenistic
Jews (even such a notable figure as Philo Judaeus, c. 20 BCE-50
CE) were seen as bastard Greek thinkers, Buddhism came to be
called one of the heterodoxies of Brahmanic-Hindu orthodoxy.
Actually, as T.R.V. Murti succinctly points out, Hinduism (based
on the *ātman*—substance or soul—doctrine of the orthodox
scriptures called the *Upanisads*) and Buddhism were two main
Indian traditions, and "they conceive reality on two distinct and
exclusive patterns."[22]

The significance of Buddhism lies in its claim that the Buddha
discovered for himself the law of liberation of all beings, so that
there is no "revealer" behind the "revelation," as it were. Buddha is
said to have uttered: "I have no teacher; none is like me; in the

world of men and spirits none is my compeer."[23] Buddha rejected the substance (*ātman*) doctrine as illusory. "There is no inner and immutable core in things; everything is in flux."[24] Thus, unlike Hindus, whose self-identity was integrally related to the earthly institution of the caste and the stages of life, early Buddhists affirmed that the *Dharma* (the liberating law for all beings) discovered by the Buddha could be realized only in the corporate life of the Buddhist community (*samgha*). Hence the three-fold formula of ancient Buddhism—*Buddham saranam gacchami* ("I take refuge in Buddha"), *Dhammam saranam gacchami* ("I take refuge in *Dharma*"), *Sangham saranam gacchami* ("I take refuge in the community"). Indeed, this three-fold affirmation often referred to as the Three Jewels, was the ancient Indian Buddhist formula of self-identity.

People in ancient China also had a clear idea of self-identity. Their "world of meaning" was defined in terms of what is often referred to as "familyism," for it was the family that was considered the norm of society, nation, and universe. Even ethics were based on the five reciprocal relationships learned in the family setting. Concretely:

1. Kindness in the father, filial piety in the son.

2. Gentility in the elder brother, humility and respect in the younger.

3. Righteous behavior in the husband, obedience in the wife.

4. Humane consideration in elders, deference in juniors.

5. Benevolence in rulers, loyalty in ministers and subjects.[25]

Once the Duke of She boasted to Confucius, saying, "In my land there is an upright man. His father stole a sheep, and the man turned him in to the authorities," whereupon Confucius is said to have replied: "The upright men of my land are different. The father will shelter the son and the son will shelter the father. Righteousness lies precisely in this."[26] Thus in ancient China, men and women, old and young, were oriented to this kind of co-operative commonwealth in which individuals knew how to talk and behave according to who they were in relation to others. A popular ballad entitled "A Woman's Hundred Years," says in part:

> At ten, like a flowering branch in the rain, she is slender, delicate, and full of grace . . . /At twenty, receiving the hairpin, she is a spring bud. Her parents arrange her betrothal; the matter's well done . . . /At thirty, perfect as a pearl, full of the beauty of youth. At her window, by the gauze curtain, she makes up in front of the mirror . . . /At forty, she is mistress of a prosperous house and makes plans. Three sons and five daughters give her some trouble . . . /At fifty, afraid of her husband's dislike, she strains to please him with every charm . . . /At sixty, face wrinkled and hair like silk thread, she walks unsteadily and speaks little . . . /At seventy, frail and thin, but not knowing what to do about it. . . .[27]

Indeed, men and women in ancient China went through various stages of life, and yet they were always rooted in their "world of meaning" which upheld the sanctity and the greater life of the family in the midst of the capriciousness of life in this phenomenal world.

It is interesting to compare India and China with a much younger nation, Japan, which nevertheless had developed and preserved its own distinct "world of meaning" in spite of the fact that it was exposed to the impact of Chinese culture at various phases of its history. From time immemorial (at least to them), the inhabitants of Japanese islands thought of their archipelago as the "world" and a sacred national community permeated by divine spirits. There in that small island kingdom people developed a multi-faceted, contradictory culture of their own, known for its emphasis on poetry as well as warriorhood. For example, the *Man'yōshū* ("Collection of Myriad Leaves"), an anthology of 4500 ancient poems, contains a touching poem of a frontier-guard as he was sent for his service in a far-off place. "Though sad is the parting from my wife/I summoned the courage of a man/and dressed for the journey, take my leave/My mother strokes me gently/My young wife clings to me, saying,/I will pray to the gods for your safe-keeping . . . / Hard as it is, I start on my way/Pausing and looking back time after time. . . ."[28] To be sure, not every young man in ancient Japan was such an upright soldier, but there is no doubt that the sense of loyalty to the sacred national community was an important facet of the historical Japanese "world of meaning."

The fact that people in historical India (both Hindus and Buddhists), China, Japan, and other parts of Asia, had a secure sense of self-identity was due to a great extent to the stability and power of their worlds of meaning. Significantly, in each case the "self" in the modern Western sense tended to be eclipsed in the larger, collectivistic self which defined the roles and statuses of the individuals involved. And throughout the long history of Asia, except in emergency situations, such historical worlds of meaning were kept alive, modified and reinterpreted by numerous *Kulturträgers* ("culture carriers") in every generation.

Cosmos, Nature, and Humankind

Circularity, the common feature of the historical worlds of meaning in various parts of Asia, was based on the correlative principles (i) between cosmos and the empirical world, (ii) between human beings and the world of nature, and (iii) between spirit and matter.

(i) Correlation between the cosmos and the empirical world.

Throughout Asia, it was widely held that the world was not created by someone or something other than itself and that the world has for all intents and purposes no beginning or end; the world simply *is*. In this world, time is a chain of ever-repeating seasons, and creation is a constant recreation. Accordingly, Easterners by and large have not acknowledged the existence of a transcendental creator-deity in their perception of the monistic universe, even though they were inclined to deify the inherent powers of everything in the celestial and terrestrial spheres. For example, in India prominent deities were believed to reside in the upper region of heaven, but a countless number of earthly deities, such as the elephant-god, the monkey-god, and the snake-god, were also venerated. In Japan, a leading thinker of the native Shinto ("the *kami* way") religion affirmed that the word *kami* ("deity," "god," or "spirit") referred to both heavenly and earthly deities; furthermore, according to him, "among all kinds of beings—including not only human beings but also such objects as birds, beasts, trees, grass, seas, mountains, and so forth—any being whatsoever which possesses some eminent quality out of the ordinary, and awe-inspiring, is called *kami*."[29] But all these deities, like human and other beings, were believed to be subservient to the regulative order or inner balance of the cosmos, whereby the power of the immanent, hidden cosmic order was believed to be regulating the movements of the stars, creating and recreating all life in the world of nature. As in the immortal verses of the *Tao Te Ching* ("The Way and Its Power"), the ancient Chinese classic put it so simply and poignantly:

> There was a formless actuality
> Before heaven and earth developed;
> Lonely, isolated,
> Independent, unchanging,
> Revolving unfailingly,
> Able to be mother of all things under heaven.
> Not knowing its name
> I call it "Tao."
> . . . .
> Man follows the earth;
> The earth follows heaven;
> Heaven follows Tao;
> Tao follows its own nature.[30]

It should not be overlooked that ancient Easterners found various kinds of close connections between the cosmos and the empirical world, or heaven and earth. For example, in ancient India people were persuaded that heaven and earth were two facets of one huge community of beings (not of things), the operation of which reflected a multi-dimensional "metaphysics." In this respect, Heimann astutely observes:

In India . . . Metaphysics never acquired the significance of "beyond" all physical facts; it has rather always been Physics. If then Indian Metaphysics is concerned with problems centering on the conception of God, that is with Theology, Metaphysics may be called "a second Physics," since God is the heavenly counterpart of earthly physical beings. If applied, again, to cosmic primeval Physics, or to Ontology, then the meaning becomes "extended Physics," while when it deals with the fate of Man after death, it is "a renewed Physics," simply because India's ideas of life after death, of the Hereafter, are those of another "here," of a new life on earth in reincarnation.[31]

Similarly, ancient Chinese cosmologists affirmed close correspondence between heaven and earth, between human psychological-physiological functions and cosmic operations, and even between "the cosmos, especially the heavens, with the dynastic state and the imperial bureaucracy."[32] Unfortunately, space does not allow us to discuss how other Asian traditions developed their own correlative principles to explain the close connections between the cosmos and the empirical world.

(ii) The inseparability of human beings and the world of nature

Obviously, by separating this section from the previous discussion of the correlation between the cosmos and the empirical world, we are trying to make it easier for those who accept Western categories to follow our portrayal of Eastern worlds of meaning. Actually, to most Easterners the above mentioned items are two sides of the same coin. It is worth noting, however, in sharp contrast to Protagoras' dictum that the human being is the measure of all things (and as such in the West it was often believed that the human being occupied an exalted place between deities and the world of nature) that the Eastern traditions assigned to the human being a humbler status as a part of the world of nature. This also implied that in the Eastern context the human being did not have a separate destiny apart from the cosmos with its seasons and changes. Thus ancient Indian sages affirmed: "This Ātman (the vital essence in Man) is the same in the ant, the same in the gnat, the same in the elephant, the same in these three worlds . . . the same in the whole universe."[33] One can readily see that such an outlook underlies the belief in the cycles or streams of existence, often called the doctrine of transmigration, in its Hindu, Jain, or Buddhist forms.

The ancient Chinese also acknowledged their profound dependence upon the world of nature. According to Wing-tsit Chan, there were at least three major theories concerning this. "The first is the theory of correspondence between man and Nature developed by the Yin Yang School; it was adopted by both the Confucian and Taoist Schools, and vastly influenced Chinese thought . . . ."[34] The second theory, according to Chan, was that of harmony (and not "submission to," as it was often misunderstood) of Nature and the human being. Even though some Confucianists also gave assent to this theory, it is usually associated with the Taoist tradition, as exemplified by Chuang Tzu's exhortation to be Nature's companion. "Chuang Tzu actually lived with Nature, for he loved to move among the deer and swines. The Neo-Taoists, especially the celebrated Seven Worthies of the Bamboo Groves of the third century A.D., went even further. . . . They were fatalists and escapists, to be sure, but in them man and Nature become completely harmonious."[35] The third major theory is that of the Confucian view of "forming a triad with Heaven and Earth," or its later reformulation of "forming one body with Heaven and Earth." It is to be noted that, with regard to this doctrine, Confucianism split between the tradition of Hsun Tzu, advocating the control of Nature, and that of Mencius, laying the chief emphasis on the human factor.[36]

Undoubtedly, the principle of the inseparability of human beings and the world of nature was graphically presented in Chinese landscape painting. Its ideal came to reflect the influence of Buddhism, too, after the T'ang period (A.D. 618-907). For example, René Grouset tells us that painters during the Sung period (A.D. 960-1279) spent much time meditating on nature. "They were to 'lay bare the spirit' and it was 'the spirit of nature' that they were to reveal to us. They were to recreate nature for us, not in an artificial and academic manner, to be sure, but so to speak metaphysically, after having purified it of its materiality (whence the abandonment of colour) by removing almost every concrete feature and retaining nothing but its hidden spirituality and its pure essence."[37]

In all of Asia, Japan first and foremost nurtured the pattern of the inseparability of human beings and nature, undoubtedly helped by its temperate climate and natural beauty (decorated by volcanic peaks, rivers, small plains, lakes, and scenic coastal lines). The inhabitants of the Japanese islands lived close to the world of nature, and this tradition became a prominent feature of the native religion called Shinto, which Langdon Warner called the "nurse of arts."[38] In this tradition, people lived with a sense of gratitude for the beneficent forces of nature.

> Natural forces are the very subject matter of those who produce artifacts from raw material or who hunt and fish and farm. Thus Shinto taught successful generations of Japanese how such forces are controlled and these formulas have become embedded in Shinto liturgies. Dealing, as this body of beliefs does, with the essence of life and with the spirits inhabiting all natural and many artificial objects, it came about that no tree could be marked off for felling, no bush tapped for lacquer juice, no oven built for smelting for pottery, and no forge fire lit without appeal to the *Kami* resident in each.[39]

Living as they did in such a simple all-embracing world of nature, the ancient Japanese took it for granted that there was no discontinuity between art and religion, or between song and prayer. This heightened awareness of the connection of the human and the natural was expressed in poetic verses, as exemplified by the *Man'yōshū*, mentioned earlier. Later on, the Chinese ink painting of the Sung tradition became a vogue among Japanese artists. The ink painting, says Warner, "manages with admirable economy, in a flick, to show a curving surface and an edge. The soft ink is coal black, or watered down to a mist of gray. It omits just as the eye omits in looking at a landscape, and the spectator brings to the scene his own image-making faculty that we all share, no two of us alike, the exercise of which is the highest creative delight."[40]

What Warner says of the Chinese ink painting can be applied to many of the Eastern worlds of meaning. People in Asia facing the uncertainties of life have long contemplated the mystery of life, without regulating the world of nature and yet without falling into fatalism. Their attitude was receptive. Nevertheless, they exercised their image-making faculty to perceive and recreate the inner fabric of life's meaning and to express it in art, religion, philosophy, music and literature (to follow the Western convention of demarcating life), as well as in interhuman relationships.

(iii) Unity of mind and body or spirit and matter

The question of the mind-body or spirit-matter relation is admittedly a universal one. Historically, Easterners have been inclined to accept spirit and matter as equally primeval principles. In fact, the Saṅkhya and Vedānta Schools in India went so far as to affirm that "it is from Matter, not from Spirit, that all cosmic and specific psychic faculties are derived; Man's intellect (*Buddhi*) is also regarded as an emanation of primeval Matter and not of Spirit."[41] Moreover, this perception fostered a belief held widely from India to Japan, that deities were powers inherent in everything in the celestial and earthly spheres. It is well known that India developed one of the most thoroughgoing systems of meditation, Yoga, which enables one to be "liberated in this life" through recovery of "the original situation enriched by the dimension of *freedom* and *transconsciousness*."[42] Such a high spiritual aim requires meticulous bodily training in "postures" (*āsana*) and "respiratory discipline" (*prāṇāyāma*).[43] By mastering physical as well as mental disciplines, the human being "creates the spiritual dimension of freedom, and 'introduces' it into the cosmos and life—that is, into blind and tragically conditioned modes of existence."[44]

Clearly Buddhism owes much to Yoga, though its soteriology is very different. According to canonical writings, the Buddha, distressed by the transience of life, devoted himself to asceticism and Yogic discipline. But, unable to find his answers, he spent nearly seven years a lonely ascetic. Eventually he abandoned asceticism, and concentrated on meditation. One night he stumbled upon the law of liberation of all beings by gaining piercing insight into the meaning of existence, thus experiencing liberation. "And in me emancipated arose the knowledge of my emancipation. I realized that destroyed is birth, the religious life has been led, done is what was to be done, there is naught [for me] beyond this world. . . . Ignorance was dispelled, knowledge arose. Darkness was dispelled, light arose."[45]

Indeed, from the moment of the Buddha's emancipatory experience onward, all Buddhists have followed his goal with the conviction that right conduct is the prerequisite for meditation and insight, which in turn are prerequisites for liberation. In time various methods and techniques of meditation developed within Buddhism. Among them, three important ones are: (i) the meditation techniques of the southern (or the Theravāda) tradition, (ii) the Tibetan form of esoteric meditation, and (iii) Ch'an/Zen as widely practiced in China and Japan. All of them regard meditation as a discipline of the total person, combining mental, spiritual, and bodily aspects, as evidenced in the "breath-and-body-mindfulness" or "body-process-awareness" method of the Theravāda,[46] the Tibetan tradition of *Mahāmudra*,[47] and *zazen* (sitting meditation) of Zen.[48]

In China, the age-old longing for liberation and for physical longevity and immortality gave rise to various Taoist formulas for coordinating body, mind, and spirit. For example, Needham mentions six classical Taoist techniques for achieving material immortality as a *hsien* (immortal)—(i) respiratory, (ii) heliotherapeutic, (iii) gymnastic, (iv) sexual, (v) alchemical and pharmaceutical, and (vi) dietary.[49] We might also classify the Taoist formulas into the two popular general categories of "outer elixir" (*wai-tan*), which usually involves the use of a drug of immortality, and "inner or esoteric elixir or alchemy" (*nei-tan*), which aims at "the refining by various means of the spiritual essence within the body in order to liberate this spiritual essence. . . ."[50] Thompson notes: "In the spiritual physiology of religious Taoism the life force was identified with such obviously vital components as breath, blood, and semen. To preserve life, these components must be conserved. . . . The peculiarity about the religious Taoist notion of breath was that it was not merely inhalation and exhalation of an exterior substance, but that it was a progressive 'using up' of the allotment of life-spirit with which one is born."[51] Significantly, Taoist practice, which requires a considerable amount of training, avoids extremes. According to a popular Taoist precept: "The art of cultivating one's

Nature is like that of playing on the strings of a musical instrument: too great a force can break the string, while too weak a pull will not produce any sound; one must find the perfect means to produce the perfect note."[52]

Other Asian traditions also developed fairly sophisticated theories regarding the balancing body and mind or matter and spirit. For example, in his recent book, Yuasa posits a theory that the apparent distinction between the mind and body in the Eastern context is not an ontological distinction. As Thomas Kasulis, the editor and a translator of Yuasa's book, states in his "Introduction," Eastern traditions "generally treat mind-body unity as an achievement, rather than an essential relation. This insight relates a number of formerly disconnected observations about Asian culture. First, it is clearer why meditation and philosophical insight are inseparable in the Eastern traditions: wisdom must be physically as well as intellectually developed. Truth is not only a way of thinking about the world; it is a mode of being in the world, part of which includes one's bodily existence. Thus, meditation and thinking are not to be separated."[53]

Thus, accepting the correlation between cosmos and the empirical world, the inseparability of human beings and the world of nature, and the unity of mind and body (or spirit and matter), as well as the subservience of all beings to the eternal regulative principles, Easterners were spared some neurotic anxieties concerning their place in the world or their destiny in life. After all, in accordance with this perspective, every being in the world of nature shares the same life regulated by the same cosmic order that exists from eternity to eternity. Who are we, mere mortals, to think of ourselves superior to other animals or plants? And when the time comes, a Japanese poet wrote:

> What a pity, O cherry blossoms, so hurriedly
> Scattering away!
> Why not follow the spirit of Spring,
> So peaceful, so relaxing, so eternally contended?[54]

In the unitary meaning structure developed in the East there was no sharp distinction between the sacred and the secular. Hence ancient Easterners were religious because they never questioned the idea that everything in the world was permeated by the Sacred, rather than because they reflected on the meaning of life in any special religious terms. In short, *living* in the historical worlds of meaning in Asia *itself* was what Westerners now call a "religious act."

Metaphysico-Social Principles

Metaphysico-social principles in the Eastern world uphold the historical conviction that the social and political order was rooted in the "natural," which in turn was identified with the "original." This reflected the prevalent, Eastern notion that empirical, social and political institutions were believed to be grounded ultimately in the sacred, cosmic order. The famous Indian "caste system" mentioned earlier is a case in point. We have read all kinds of arguments against the evil of separating castes in all aspects of life, e.g., in marriage, eating, residence, occupation, and religious worship. Worst of all, the treatment of the so-called untouchables or the "scheduled class" shocks many outsiders. But, according to many Hindus, the caste system is more than a system of social stratification; it reflects the cosmic order. "In the sacramental order," said Ananda K. Coomaraswamy, "there is need and a place for all men's work: and there is no more significant consequence of the principle, Work is Sacrifice, than the fact that under these conditions, and remote as this may be from our secular way of thinking, every function, from that of the priest and the king down to that of potter and scavenger, is literally a priesthood and every operation a rite."[55]

Similarly, other socio-political patterns, e.g., the family system in China and the national community in Japan, have been regarded as reflections of the sacred order of the universe. The sacrality of the Chinese family (*chia*) is particularly well-known. It is not simply an important unit of social cohesion, consisting of a father, a mother, their sons and unmarried daughters, the sons' wives and children, and so forth; it is a paradigmatic norm for social, political, and religious orders. Moreover, not only living members belong to the family; the deceased and those who are yet to come are considered to be integral parts of the family. Hence the importance of genealogy, ancestor veneration, the practice of mourning, memorial services and other family cults. In China, for example, a typical genealogy starts the family tree with the earliest known ancestor. Then "the first section lists the five generations from him to his great-great-grandson, the next section lists the next five generations, and then the next five generations, and so on. Thus, starting from the outer branches, one can trace the ultimate origin of one's heritage; starting at the beginning, one can survey the development of the branches."[56] Inevitably, the family system over several generations produces an extended family or kinship group. Subsequently, the intra-family relations are handled through, among other things, the system of the five degrees of mourning (*wu fu*), which in effect means "the five kinds of mourning which, in descending order of duration and severity corresponding to the closeness of kinship, are to be observed by any given members of a family upon the death of any other members."[57]

The status of living individuals is defined in terms of their respective standing in the family, and their social status is determined to a great extent by the prestige of their family. Because the nation was often understood to be modelled after the family, many emperors portrayed themselves as the father of the national family. When Buddhism was transplanted to China, it had to vigorously refute the charge that the act of men and women joining the Buddhist orders was contrary to the family ethics of filial piety, and it had to develop various rites for ancestral worship."[58]

In many cases, religious myths and symbols were utilized to uphold the metaphysico-social principles in various parts of Asia. The Shinto myths in Japan supported the claim of the imperial clan that the Japanese emperors, being genealogical descendants of the sun deity (Amaterasu Ōmikami, the tutelary deity of the imperial family), were the combinations of the living *kami*, the sacred king, the high priest. Accordingly it was decreed in the seventh century that the high government officials were to assemble at 4:00 a.m. on every working day outside the south gate of the imperial court to be admitted to the inner court exactly at sunrise in order to pay homage to the sovereign, descendant of the sun deity. Only after this homage was performed were they expected to attend to administrative duties.[59] Undoubtedly such stylized court rituals were meant to be the earthly replica of heavenly rituals told in Shinto myths.

Another example is that of the fifteenth century reform ruler of Sukhotai, the kingdom in what is now Thailand, who utilized a combination of ancient Hindu concepts and Buddhist myths. He believed that the function of the ruler was

> to harmonize activities on earth with the cosmic forces of the universe. This was achieved by organizing the kingdom as a universe in miniature: the king's palace represented the sacred Mount Meru, city of the gods, while his four chief ministers corresponded to the guardian deities of the four cardinal points of the universe. The capital itself stood for the whole country.[60]

Thus certain metaphysico-social principles, religious or otherwise, upheld the historical Eastern worlds of meaning through many generations.

Erosion of historical Eastern worlds of meaning

The Eastern worlds of meaning and their "communities" (those intricate homologies of religious and non-religious dimensions) achieved a high degree of communication of religious and cultural values, to the extent that they appeared to the community members to be self-evident. Such Asian communities remind us of the classical features of *Gemeinschaft*, "something not manufactured, but given; it depends not upon sentiment or feeling, but on the Unconscious. It need be founded upon no conviction, since it is self-evident; we do not become members of it, but 'belong to it.' "[61]

One important characteristic of the Eastern communities was the amazing number of people who played important roles in transmitting their worlds of meaning from generation to generation. In fact, it was taken for granted in historical Asia that *Kulturträgers* were ideally ordinary men and women, engaged in trade, farming, government service or fishing as well as poetry, dramatics, painting, literature, and philosophical and religious reflections. Even among the famous gentry-scholars (*Ju*), who spent many years studying for government services in historical China, there were many who never accepted official positions. Nevertheless, they epitomized the Eastern ideal of being learned members of society who had mastered the sacred knowledge of the past and could transmit it to the present generation, guarding revered institutions and interpreting contemporary experiences in the light of accumulated wisdom. In this, they followed the admonition of Confucius himself.

> A Ju lives with the moderns but studies with the ancient. What he does today will become an example for the generations to follow. When he lives in times of political chaos, he neither courts favors from those in authority, nor is boosted by those below. And when the petty politicians join hands to defame or injure him, his life may be threatened, but the course of his conduct may not be changed. Although he lives in danger, his soul remains his own. And even then he does not forget the sufferings of the people.[62]

Such high ideals of Confucius notwithstanding, many gentry-scholars found it more convenient and profitable to uphold the status quo, catering to the powerful at the expense of the welfare of the less fortunate. Inevitably, with the increasing stratification of society, more institutional divisions of professional groups appeared in addition to such old establishments as clerics, soldiers, and eunuchs. The growing division of society that resulted made it difficult for the Eastern communities to maintain their ideals, i.e., the integration of all cultural values and the balancing and harmonizing of the diverse groups within them. Yet it is remarkable that the Eastern worlds of meaning persisted as long as they did, a fact partly due to their "religious" underpinning. "Religion" in the Eastern context was not what has come to be accepted by Westerners—one facet of life, existing alongside politics, art, law, economics, etc. Historically, Easterners never used such terms as religion, but they affirmed that all facets of life share the same invisible sacred foundation. Indeed, we may use the term "religion" to refer to that comprehensive affirmation of ancient Asians. Obviously, various festivities and communal rituals not only solidified the organic unity of historical Eastern communities but also communicated the deeper sanctions of existence. Thus, by participating in "religious" activities, e.g., festivals, pilgrimages and holy days, the ancient Asians re-enacted certain memorable and decisive communal experiences.

Eventually, however, approximately five centuries ago the once intact Eastern worlds of meaning and their underlying metaphysico-social principles gradually began to erode. If we might pinpoint dates, we might depict the establishment of (i) the Mughal dynasty in India (1526), (ii) the Tokugawa feudal regime in Japan (1603), and (iii) the Manchu (Ch'ing) dynasty in China (1644). Ironically, despite the best intentions of the Mughal dynasty, the Tokugawa regime, and the Manchu dynasty to preserve the culture, Indian, Japanese, and Chinese society became regimented by top-heavy administrative machines, determined to preserve the forms but unable to nurture the spirit of their worlds of meaning.

Notes

1 Harold Isaacs, *Scratches on the Mind* (New York: John Day, 1958), 39.

2 See Kitagawa, *American Refugee Policy*.

3 Henri de Lubac, *La recontre du Bouddhisme et de l'Occident* (Paris: Aubier Editions Montaigne, 1952), 274, FN 46.

4 Hendrik Kraemer, *World Cultures and World Religions* (Philadelphia: The Westminster Press, 1960), 18.

5 M.E. Cameron, "Far Eastern Studies in the U.S.," *The Far Eastern Quarterly*, VII:2 (February 1948), 119-20.

6 R.M. Hutchins, *The Great Conversation*, in *Great Books of the Western World* (17 vols; Chicago: Encyclopedia Britannica, 1951), I, 72-73.

7 *Ibid.*, 63.

8 W.S. Haas, *The Destiny of the Mind: East and West* (London: Faber and Faber, 1956), 14.

9 *Ibid.*, 15-16.

10 Oswald Spengler, *The Decline of the West* (2 vols.; New York: A.A. Knopf, 1930), II, 57.

11 F.S.C. Northrop, *The Meeting of East and West* (New York: Macmillan, 1946), 312.

12 Mircea Eliade, *Myths, Dreams and Mysteries* (New York: Harper and Row, 1960), 8-9.

13 Betty Heimann, *Indian and Western Philosophy: A Study of Contrasts* (London: G. Allen and Unwin, 1937), 27.

14 Lily Abegg, *The Mind of East Asia* (London: Thames and Hudson, 1952).

15 *Ibid.*, 32.

16 *Ibid.*, 213.

17 Yu-Kuang Chu, "The Liberal Values of Non-Western Studies," reprinted from *TOPIC: The Journal of the Liberal Arts* (Washington, Pennsylvania: Washington and Jefferson College, 1962), 10.

18 William Earle, *Public Sorrows and Private Pleasures* (Bloomington: Indiana University Press, 1976), 75.

19 Swami Nikhilananda, "Hindu Ethics," in R.N. Anshen, ed., *Moral Principles of Action* (New York: Harper and Row, 1952), 621.

20 *Ibid.*, 619.

21 *Ibid.*, 620-21.

22 T.R.V. Murti, *The Central Philosophy of Buddhism* (London: G. Allen and Unwin, 1955), 10.

23 Quoted in J.G. Jennings, *The Vedantic Buddhism of Buddha* (London: Oxford University Press, 1948), 66.

24 Murti, *Philosophy of Buddhism*, 10.

25 Cited in J.A. Hutchinson, *Paths of Faith* (New York: McGraw-Hill, 1969), 213-214.

26 Quoted in Patricia B. Ebrey, ed., *Chinese Civilization and Society: A Sourcebook* (New York: Macmillan, 1981), 16.

27 Quoted in *ibid.*, 56.

28 I used the translation of Nihon Gakujutsu Shinkokai, *The Manyōshū*, reissued by Columbia University Press in 1965, 175.

29 Cited in Shigeru Matsumoto, *Motoori Norinanga 1730-1801* (Cambridge: Harvard University Press, 1970), 84.

30 *Tao Te Ching*, chapter 25. I am using the translation of Constant C.C. Chang and W.H. Forthman, cited in J.W. Dye and W.H. Forthman, *Religions of the*

World: Selected Readings (New York: Appleton Century Crofts, 1957), 247-248.

31 Heimann, *Indian and Western Philosophy*, 29-30.

32 John B. Henderson, *The Development and Decline of Chinese Cosmology* (New York: Columbia University Press, 1984), 5.

33 *Bṛhadāranyaka-upaniṣad* I, 3, 22; cited in the frontal page of Heimann, *Indian and Western Philosophy*.

34 Wing-tsit Chan, "The Concept of Man in Chinese Thought," in S. Radhakrishnan and P.T. Raju, eds., *The Concept of Man* (London: G. Allen and Unwin, 1960), 211.

35 *Ibid.*, 213.

36 *Ibid.*, 214.

37 René Grouset, *Chinese Art and Culture* (New York: Grove Press, 1959), 250.

38 Langdon Warner, *The Enduring Art of Japan* (Cambridge: Harvard University Press, 1952), 17.

39 *Ibid.*, 18-19.

40 *Ibid.*, 57.

41 Heimann, *Indian and Western Philosophy*, 40.

42 Mircea Eliade, *Yoga: Immortality and Freedom* (Bollingen Series, LVI; New York: Pantheon Books, 1958), 99.

43 Ibid., 53-59.

44 Ibid., 100.

45 Contained in *The Padhana-sutta from the Sutta-nipata*, trans. Lord Chalmers, in *Buddha's Teaching*, Harvard Oriental Series, XXXVII, 68.

46 See W.L. King, *A Thousand Lives Away: Buddhism in Contemporary Burma* (Cambridge: Harvard University Press, 1964), chapter VI, "The More Excellent Way," 180-219.

47 See Chang Chen-chi, *The Practice of Zen* (New York: Harper and Row, 1959), 170, FN 1.

48 See Chan, *The Great Asian Religions*, 288.

49 Joseph Needham, *Science and Civilization in China* (London: Cambridge University Press, 1956), II, 143.

50 L.G. Thompson, *Chinese Religion: An Introduction* (Belmont: Dickenson, 1969), 90.

51 *Ibid.*, 94.

52 Ebrey, *Chinese Civilization*, 77.

53 Thomas Kasulis, "Editor's Introduction" to *The Body: Toward an Eastern Mind-Body Theory* by Yuasa Yasuo (Albany: State University of New York Press, 1987), 3-4.

54 Written by Fujiwara Toshinari, 1114-1204; cited in D.T. Suzuki, *Zen and Japanese Culture* (Bollingen Series, LXIV, New York: Pantheon Books, 1959), 390.

55 A.K. Coomaraswamy, *Hinduism and Buddhism* (New York: Philosophical Library, 1943), 6.

56 Quoted in Ebrey, *Chinese Civilization*, 237.

57 Derk Bodde, *Essays on Chinese Civilization* (Princeton: Princeton University Press, 1981), 168.

58 Kenneth K.S. Ch'en, *The Chinese Transformation of Buddhism* (Princeton: Princeton University Press, 1973) chapter II, "Ethical Life."

59 J.M. Kitagawa, "The Japanese *Kokutai* [National Community]: History and Myth," *History of Religions*, 13:3 (February 1974), 222.

60 J.L.S. Girling, *Thailand: Society and Politics* (Ithaca: Cornell University Press, 1981), 22.

61 G. van der Leeuw, *Religion in Essence and Manifestation* (London: G. Allen and Unwin, 1938), 243.

62 Lin Yutang, ed. and trans., *The Wisdom of Confucius* (New York: Random House, 1938), 6.

Chapter Two

Mutual Image: European and Asian

Ancient World

Around 1970 the Filipino scholar-statesman Carlos Romulo stated that the mysterious, remote, other-worldly Asia is a creation of the Western mind, a mind incapable of fitting the seamlessness of the Eastern world into neatly demarcated Western categories. Conversely, as I once stated after one of my trips to Asia:

> I encountered a number of equally one-sided, superficial, and partially correct, views about the 'West.' To many Asians, Europeans were the villains of now discredited colonialism, and unhappily Americans are now blamed for the sins of their European cousins. How often I tried, not successfully I am afraid, to bring variety to their impression that Easterners are spiritual, while Westerners are materialistic, sex-conscious, and gadget-happy. To those Asians who were otherwise convinced, it was a losing battle to point out that Hollywood movies and the Kinsey Report are not the most reliable guides for judging Western culture. For example, some of them had a mental image of America in which [Blacks] are beaten everyday. Orientals are confined to concentration camps, Indians were massacred, and policemen are crooks. ...[1]

It is, of course, always a mystery how people arrive at important decisions or judgments. I am sure that those who have watched the Watergate or Iran-Contra hearings on TV screens cannot help but wonder how some of those seemingly rational human beings come to such diametrically opposed conclusions based, presumably, on the same evidence. What seems to be involved in all these cases is an uncanny process of coordinating our "knowledge," based on information, with our "attitude," which usually embraces both our premise as well as our manner of adjusting to new knowledge (e.g., degrees of flexibility or openness to alter our premise in the light of newly acquired knowledge about certain facts or information). To put it more concretely, when our premise is so firm or we think we already know all the answers, no new knowledge will change our views. If, on the other hand, we are confused and tentative or highly susceptible to new knowledge, (which tends to annihilate our preconceived notions altogether), we are bound to change our views or stances constantly. Unhappily, there are far too many of those who change their minds too often and those who have very closed minds—fanatics, due to their premature exposure to, say, certain kinds of excessive religious or military institutions. (Unfortunately, we must recognize that a *normal* maturing process, involving a wholesome balance of "knowledge," "attitude," with some needed dose of skepticism, is becoming increasingly more difficult in today's world.)

One of the most common phenomena of group relations is the practice of "typing" people, often in sharp dichotomy. The diaries and letters of many Westerners who lived in the non-Western world during the colonial period—government officials, military personnel, missionaries and businessmen—betray how pervasive such practices were. Most of them portrayed themselves as for the most part civilized, honest, hard-working, fair, generous, kind, and reasonable, whereas the non-Whites with whom they dealt were superstitious, dishonest, lazy, cunning, ungrateful, cruel, and irrational. Many Easterners who resented being ruled by colonial regimes indulged in similar oversimplifications — only reversing them. (A similar phenomenon happened frequently in inter-group relations in American society.)

Such crude "typing" and "categorizing" between the Westerner and the Easterner is not an old phenomenon. It commenced gradually in the West and in the East, together with the growing sense of ethnocentric and culture-bound self-identity. In the West, the European "world of meaning" and the "metaphysico-social principles" were only gradually homologized in the huge, unified framework of the ecclesiastically controlled medieval synthesis. Yet, even after its secularization, expedited by the Renaissance and the

Enlightenment, and in spite of the determined efforts of the secularists to the contrary, the European synthesis did not lose its "religious" character completely. It advocated the absolutistic gospel of secularized salvation, e.g., scientific determinism, evolutionism, human freedom (more "civil" than "political," however), democracy, capitalism, progress and modernization. Confronted by the strong influence of the West, the reactions of the East for its part were not unified—in keeping with the traditional acceptance of juxtaposition, which meant the recognition of several, autonomous religious-cultural-social political syntheses, including the Western. In the next chapter, we will discuss how the "absolutist" Western outlook impinged itself upon the "relativist" and diversified Eastern world during the past four centuries. In this chapter, we will briefly analyze the prior and more elementary picture, that is, how different cultural orbits in the ancient world developed and intermingled.

Cosmic Legitimations

No definitive statements have been made regarding the origins of civilization, but many would agree with Herbert Muller's general statement that "material wealth and power are essentially only the basis, the means to other ends. . . . The creation and transmission of the spiritual achievements of a society depend upon its material achievements; its monuments testify to both its artistic and its technological power, its ideals and wealth."[2] The essential need for material resources and a comfortable climate might explain the emergence, within a relatively short span of time starting around 3500 B.C., of the great river-valley civilizations of the ancient world, such as the (i) Mesopotamian, (ii) Egyptian, (iii) Indus Valley, and (iv) early Chinese, all in the north temperate zone in one continuous land-area of Eurasia. All of them went through similar processes, such as gradual passage from an age of stone, then that of bronze, and finally one of iron. It is almost uncanny, as Carl W. Bishop points out, how all these civilizations were based on "identically the set of fundamental elements: the knowledge of copper or bronze, town-building, the use of wheeled vehicles, possession of the common domestic animals, the growing of certain cereals, especially wheat, and the idea of writing, in one form or another. Nowhere else did this group of culture-traits occur in similar combination. . . ."[3]

There is no question that the numerous racial and cultural groups in the ancient world must have had their sense of corporate "we-consciousness" in relation to neighboring or rival groups and visitors and slaves within their borders. Such a vague sense of "we-consciousness," which all groups share, became a more self-conscious and all-inclusive—almost self-evident—conviction of "self-identity" when the cultural-and-religious tradition and social-and-political structure intersected so that the former authenticated the latter and vice versa. This is exemplified by the merging of the ancient Jewish religious-and-cultural tradition and the tribal-based monarchy in the form of the Davidic Kingdom around the tenth century B.C. in accordance with the Prophet Samuel's blueprint. Significantly, roughly between 500-200 B.C. several great empires emerged—the Persian under Darius the Great (548-486 B.C.), the Hellenistic (Macedonian) under Alexander the Great (356-323 B.C.), the Indian under Candragupta Maurya (321-298 B.C.) and his grandson, the "Buddhist King," Aśoka (264-223 B.C.), and the Chinese under Shih Huang-ti (the "First Emperor"—259-210 B.C.) of the Ch'in dynasty. All these empires synthesized their respective religious-cultural-social-political syntheses and in so doing "domesticated" the components of religion. In effect, they sought mainly cosmic legitimation of the self-identity of the people, who were now, roughly speaking, divided along "imperial" lines.

*   *   *   *   *

The development of a seamless synthesis of religious-cultural-social-political orders, bound to be a self-authenticating system, gave each empire a self-righteous claim for its cause. The uniqueness of different religious traditions was not a crucial factor in every case. For example, Darius the Great, who adhered to Zoroastrianism as a national religion, often invoked the Zoroastrian deity Ahuramazda in his inscriptions, mainly as a benefactor—"by the grace of Ahuramazda"—to him as "great king, king of kings, king of lands, king of this earth. . . ."[4] But we learn nothing about even the main tenets of Zoroastrianism—its eschatology, its monotheism and ethical dualism, etc.—from Darius's reference to Zoroastrianism. Although he was no doubt a devotee of Zoroastrianism, its unique religious features did not concern him. (There is good reason to believe that when he was in Egypt he venerated the Egyptian deity, Amon. We also know that in 519 he authorized Jews to rebuild the Temple for themselves in Jerusalem, and we are told that he handsomely contributed to the Greek sanctuaries as well.) Even when a specific religious tradition was preferred, that fact in itself did not dispel other religious claims or other religious-cultural-social-political syntheses. For example, King Aśoka was known for his fervent devotion to Buddhism, and he was instrumental in establishing an eclectic Buddhist-Hindu system as a bulwark of his empire. Yet, he also venerated other traditions, such as the Brāhmanas, Śramanas, Ājīvikas, and the Jains.[5]

Divine-Human Savior Motif

In the West, the "divine-human-savior image" is added to the usual, familiar equation of the religious-cultural-social-political synthesis. This image developed gradually in the West at the convergence of Zoroastrian-Jewish-Greek (especially Alexander's)-Roman-Christian insights. According to Zoroastrianism, the deity created the spiritual and the material worlds and expects human beings to cooperate with God in fighting against evil until the appearance of the last savior and judge, Saošyant, who will rehabilitate the whole creation. Under the impact of Zoroastrian eschatology, the Hebrew community after the Babylonian exile developed what has come to be known as "ethical monotheism," with a strong consciousness of being an elected ("chosen") and covenanted community. The Hebrew "peoplehood" meant that the Jewish people constituted a holy people "made holy by a holy

God."[6] This, however, was not simply a human community under God's commandment. As Muilenburg astutely observes: "the nature of Israel's moral accountability and responsibility is understood in reference to the nature of God. God is LORD of the community yet in some sense *a member of the community.* He participated actively in its life, maintains his relationship to it, and assumes the responsibility of one who is in covenant with his people." He 'loves justice, hates robbery and iniquity' (Isaiah 61:8); as Judge of all the earth he does justly (*mishpat*) (Genesis 18:25); he maintains his holiness through justice and righteousness (Isaiah 5:16)."[7] Some of the prophets realized that it was the destiny of the Hebrew community—a sort of "corporate savior"—to be a suffering servant: "he was wounded for our transgressions, he was bruised for our iniquities. . . ." (Isaiah 53: 5-6). But the Jews were exhorted not to lose faith in their God: "Keep justice, and do righteousness, for soon my salvation will come. . . ." (Isaiah 56: 1-2). Later, the motif of the "divine-human savior" was given prominence by Christianity.

With the appearance of Alexander the Great (356-323 B.C.) the map of much of the world was redrawn. An astute military ruler and stategist, he managed to establish a vast empire during his short life, encompassing Egypt, Greece, Persia and the borders of India. Also, as a one-time disciple of Aristotle, he was proud of Greek culture. In fact, he initiated a new form of colonialism, based on Hellenistic culture and the Greek (*koine*) language. No doubt Alexander's exposure to Egyptian ideology strongly influenced his image of himself as a savior and benefactor of the human race. Of course, even without Egyptian influence, the idea of savior or savior god was fairly common in those days. Cartlidge and Dungan tell us: "The Greco-Roman world, in general, held conceptions of two different kinds of Savior Gods. One type, including such Gods as Herakles, Asklepios, and Dionysos, were offspring of divine-human unions who had performed outstanding feats of benefaction (*euergesia*) on behalf of the human race, and so they were rewarded with immortality, and worshipped as Saviors. . . . The second general notion of Savior Gods was that great leaders, especially kings, were in fact temporary manifestations or appearances (*epiphaneia*) of the eternal Gods themselves. . . ."[8] We are also told that some philosophers, such as the fifth century B.C. thinker Empedocles, considered themselves to be Gods and Saviors.[9] At any rate, Alexander was an important link between the Persian empire which preceded him and the Roman empire which succeeded him as well as between Greek and Latin culture. Undoubtedly, Alexander's conquest of Palestine in 332 B.C. accelerated the trend toward Hellenistic Judaism which was destined to provide the cultural background for the birth of the Christian community. And eventually, by making Christianity the official religion of the empire under Emperor Theodosius (A.D. 346-395), Rome aspired to inherit all the important insights of Zoroastrianism, Judaism, Christianity and other religious traditions known to them as well as Persian, Egyptian, Hellenistic and Latin culture.

Europe and the Orient

Ancient peoples in various parts of the Eurasian continent had a great deal of contact among themselves. Following Alexander's Indian campaign, for instance, a series of Greek principalities in Bactria developed near the north-western borders of India. With the gradual crystallization of religious-cultural-social-political syntheses under the aegis of great civilizations, relations among peoples resembled relations among different civilization-blocs—each claiming to be the universal community of the entire known world (*oecumene*). Of course, people in each civilization-bloc were exceedingly curious about others (both foreigners and alien groups within their borders), a fact attested to by the writings of Herodotus (c. 485-425 B.C.) and Plotinus (A.D. 205-270). Some contacts between civilizations brought about mutual cultural influences. Thus, according to Basham: "Through the Greco-Bactrian kingdoms Western theories of astrology and medicine began to enter India, and perhaps the Sanskrit drama was in part inspired from this source. . . . One of the Greek kings of the Panjāb [Milinda or Menander] is especially remembered . . . as the patron of the philosopher-monk Nāgasena. . . . Thus, some of the Greeks, while not completely merging with the Indian population, soon felt the influence of their ways of thought, and made many compromises with their culture."[10] Conversely, through the inter-cultural contacts in Northwest India, the Zoroastrian belief of the savior, called Saošyant "who at the end of the world, will lead the forces of good and light against those of evil and darkness," influenced India, leading to the development of the future Buddha, Maitreya. Again, according to Basham, "around the beginning of the Christian era, the cult of the future Buddha, Maitreya, was widespread among all Buddhist sects."[11]

It is fascinating to realize that ancient Romans called the area east of the Mediterranean the "Orient," implying, to quote Webster, "the part of the horizon where the sun first appears in the morning." We can only speculate why Asia came to be referred to as the Orient, a term possessing connotations of brightness or luminosity. In any case, the existence of the ancient overland as well as the maritime trade-routes must have helped the relations of European-Chinese and European-Indian-and-Southeast Asian civilizations in cultural and scientific exchange.[12] It is no wonder that Cicero (106-43 B.C.) was deeply concerned with the impact of Chinese financial policy over the economic welfare of Rome. Frederick Teggart, studying Roman-Chinese relations from 58 B.C. to A.D. 107, notes "of the forty occasions on which outbreaks [of war] took place in Europe, twenty-seven were traceable to the policy, or rather changes of policy, of the Han [Chinese] government."[13]

The first few centuries in the Christian era provided an opportunity for the various civilizations to consolidate, although each experienced what might be called "growing pains."

In China, the magnificent Han period (202 B.C.-A.D. 220) gave way to the political disunity of the Wei, Chin, and Northern and Southern Dynasties (A.D. 220-581). By the sixth century Buddhism, which had been introduced to China during the Han, had been "naturalized" and become an important Chinese tradition, while indigenous traditions, e.g., Confucianism and Taoism, were transformed by the eclectic mood of the Han. By the time China was reunified in the Sui dynasty (A.D. 581-618), it was solidly grounded in the "multi-value system," balancing Confucianism, Taoism, and Buddhism. Indeed, from the sixth century onward the multi-value system remained a major feature of Chinese civilization.

In India, the Mauryan dynasty disintegrated shortly after the death of the Buddhist king, Aśoka, at around 232 B.C. It was destined to go through an upsetting period, characterized by invasions from outside and short-lived native dynasties both in the North and the South. During the long "Middle Ages" in the Indian subcontinent, the Sanskrit civilization of Indo-Aryans penetrated the whole of the sub-continent, sorting out many features of its cultural-religious traditions. For example, according to Thomas Hopkins: "The Purāṇas [Hindu sacred books of myths and legends] written before the fifth century A.D. reflect only the first stages in the growth of the Hindu synthesis. Temples, scarcely mentioned in these Purāṇas, became a major focus of interest in later Purāṇic writings. New forms of worship were developed. . . . Differences between Śaivite and Vaiṣnavite sects became more pronounced. . . . Worship of female deities, long practiced at the popular or village level, entered the mainstream. . . ."[14] By far the most important feature of the Hindu religious-cultural-social-political synthesis was the so-called *Varṇāśrama-dharma* system which links the *varṇa* (one's position in the cosmic cycle of transmigration) with the *āśramas* (one's development through the four stages of life). This system has remained the bulwark of Indian civilization.

In Europe, Christianity became the state religion of the Roman Empire which was later divided into the Latin and Byzantine kingdoms. After the fall of Western Rome in 476, Christendom experienced waves of barbarian invasions and a power struggle between ecclesiastical and political leaders. Christian Europe, despite its chronic internal disunity, managed each area in Western and Northern peripheries but never gained firm control of the Middle East. The phenomenon might account for the rise of Parthians (ca. 250 B.C.-ca. A.D. 230) and its overthrow by the Sāsānian dynasty (ca. A.D. 230-651).

In the European-Asian trade contacts, Europeans were particularly interested in securing Chinese silk through the overland
route, via Tarim Basin to Antioch. This trade, however, had to
utilize the Parthians (and later Sāsānians) as middlemen. The
maritime route via the Indian ocean was meant to by-pass the
Parthians and Sāsānians. The Roman appetite for luxury items
from Asia sent sailors not only to India (especially the Tamil
territories) and Ceylon, but also to Burma, Malaya, and China.
According to Basham, Roman merchants and seamen knew India
well, and "there survives a remarkable seaman's guide, compiled in
Greek by an anonymous author toward the end of the 1st century
A.D."[15] Although the importation of silk worms to Constantinople
eventually reduced the European demand for Chinese silk,
vigorous trade for other items continued to flourish between
Europe and Asia. This was bound to change, however, with the
rise of Islam in the seventh century, as we shall discuss presently.

Civilization and Religion

Both civilization and religion are Western terms with many
shades of meaning. According to Webster, civilization refers to "a
state of social culture characterized by relative progress in the arts,
science, and statecraft; also the progressive development of these
and of the means of expressing the aspirations of the human spirit,
as in art or religion." It further states that "civilization applies to
human society, and designates an advanced state of material and
social well-being, [whereas] culture, as applied to society, empha-
sizes the intellectual aspect of civilization." As to religion, Winston
King frankly acknowledges that "the very attempt to define *religion*,
to find some distinctive or possibly unique essence or set of qualities that distinguishes the 'religious' from the remainder of human
life, is primarily a Western concern." He goes on to say that "in
Asian traditions that emphasize immanence rather than transcendence, characterized by continuums rather than discontinuities
both of theory and of experience, gradations of both understanding
and of experience exist nonetheless. Recognized levels of practice

and attainment are buttressed by texts and incorporated into systems of praxis."[16] In so far as these admittedly Western terms are used in dealing with Western and Eastern situations, we must make every effort to do justice to the way each distinct tradition demarcates human experience.

Religion has the potential—even in the West—of becoming part of a seamless religious-cultural-social-political synthesis under the aegis of a civilization or an empire for which it provides cosmic legitimation. The orientation and tenets of a religion have profound implications for the self-understanding of the synthesis to which it belongs. The self-understanding of the synthesis can then serve as the basis for assessing others. In addition, some civilizations can be influenced by "foreign" religious orientations (Japan is a good example of this), which often results in misunderstanding among both insiders and outsiders.

Briefly stated, the world of meaning of the ancient Japanese was a simple unitary meaning-structure. They lived close to the world of nature, which to them was a community of beings, not things. As I once stated: "There is every indication that the early Japanese affirmed life in this world, in spite of or even because of its transitoriness, as essentially good (*yoshi*) and beautiful (*uruwashi*) [which incidentally] were almost synonymous terms. . . . This may account for the easy fusion and homology of the aesthetic and religious experiences that have given a distinctive character to the Japanese religious tradition."[17]   This simple ancient Japanese world of meaning, derived from the "particularistic" experience of the Japanese archipelago, was influenced from the fifth and sixth centuries onward by both the advanced, "alien," and "universalistic" Chinese religious-and-cultural traditions and Buddhism. But the Chinese traditions, e.g. Confucianism, Taoism and the Yin-Yang School, and Buddhism did not long remain alien. All of them, together with the indigenous Japanese Shinto tradition ("the *Kami* way") became integral parts of the religious-cultural-social-political synthesis of Japanese civilization. Interestingly, none of these traditions were "exclusivistic," a fact which might account for the religiously irenic and relativistic temper of Japanese civilization.

Western Pattern

In sharp contrast to the Japanese case, which had many significant affinities with other Asian patterns, the development in the West exhibited a strong tendency toward organic unity. This can be seen in the development of Near Eastern religious traditions, Hellenistic culture and Roman jurisprudence. Unlike the Japanese situation wherein the various religious tradition developed a "division of labor" among themselves, in the West only one religious tradition of the many which were known in the Mediterranean world became *the* religious component of the late Roman synthesis. The dominance of the Christian tradition became a matter of public record when Constantine the Great (A.D. c. 274-337) issued the edict of Milan in 313, giving civil rights to Christians.

Like the origins of many other religions, the beginning of Christianity was surrounded by numerous "histories," pious myths and legends so that a dozen adherents might give a dozen different accounts of its origin. According to the Book of Acts, the disciples of Jesus were discouraged and scattered after his crucifixion; a small group of disciples remained in Jerusalem, wondering what to do. The Christian "church" was born there by the miraculous intervention of the divine spirit—described variously as a sort of "mighty wind" or as "tongues of fire"—which caused the disciples to "speak in tongues." No doubt, anyone reading the Book of Acts will be haunted by the question of whether its account of the Pentecost, like that of the Exodus in the Hebrew Bible, portrayed a "historical" or a "religious" event.

The Book of Acts' account of Pentecost has several features which remained important to Christianity, although they may have been forgotten by many Christians. One such theme is the insistence that the Christian community was not merely a gathering of those who liked the teachings of Jesus but was meant to be the "restoration of the kingdom of Israel," interpreted not biologically or ethnically but spiritually. Secondly, the Book of Acts, like the Gospels, holds that Jesus' mission was not the political restoration of the Davidic kingdom but the eschatological restoration of the convenantal community; this was the real meaning of the statement that he was "sent to the lost sheep of the house of Israel" (Matthew 15:24). Persuaded that the spiritual covenant included the Gentiles as well as Jews, the Apostle Paul uttered the same theme: "If you are Christ's, then you are Abraham's offspring. . . ." (Galatians 3:29). Even Peter, the Jewish Christian *par excellence*, declared Jesus to be the fulfillment of the new universalistic covenant mentioned by Joel (Joel 2:28 and 30). Thus, the Book of Acts affirms that the Christian community, as was the physical extension of the Hebrew religious community, represents the reversal of the legendary account of the Tower of Babel since the scattered and broken human race is given the opportunity to be reunited as one people through divine intervention. (Such was the Book of Acts' "Christian interpretation" of the covenant, which I am sure the Jews would not accept.)

The subtle claims of the early Christian community, as exemplified by the accounts of the Book of Acts, the Gospels, and the Apostle Paul, were conducive to misunderstanding. Two issues in particular—judging from the controversies which have persisted throughout Christian history—are worth mentioning. The first is the universal-vs.-particular, and the second is the eschatological understanding of salvation vs. the conviction of salvation as a *fait accompli*, (which has come to be known in our century as the theory of *einmalchkeit*).

As to the first, the Pauline notion of the formerly ethnic Hebrew covenanted community now serving as the instrument for universal salvation was not easily understood either by Jewish or Gentile Christians. Moreover, Paul's realistic recognition that Christianity, which has to be faithful to its monotheistic faith, is but one among many religions in the Mediterranean world of his time baffled some of the faithful. But he was persuaded that: "if there are so-called Gods, whether in Heaven or on the earth—indeed there are many such Gods and many Lords—*but to us there is one God, the Father,. . . and one Lord, Jesus Christ*" (I Corinthians 8:5-6; my italics). It is interesting to compare Paul's view with the intemperate and simplistic opinion of Irenaeus (c. A.D. 130-c. 200), sometime bishop of

Lyons, who in his *Against Heresies* insisted that only Christianity is a genuine religion, while other religions are false, heretical, evil-minded, and hypocritical, and there is nothing we learn from others about the truth which we cannot easily obtain from Christianity.[18]

The change of status of Christianity from the persecuted minority to the state church of the Roman empire in the early fourth century entailed a loss of its eschatological orientation in favor of a this-worldly orientation. This led to Christianity exerting its influence without any restraint as the most powerful, earthly ecclesiastical institution. It now reflects, in the words of Peter Brown, "the attitude of a group confident of its powers to absorb the world."[19] It was but natural, then, that this kind of Christianity—authoritarian, self-righteous, this-worldly, and bureaucratic, a far cry from the Book of Acts, the Gospels and the Apostle Paul—fostered a narrow-minded and this-worldly European religious-cultural-social-political synthesis which was given presumably some sort of divine sanction. "This was," so Talcott Parsons states, "a classic case of success threatening the deeper foundations of the values for which the original great commitments were made."[20]

Although Christianity had lost its original eschatological temper, this-worldly Christianity as a state religion made a contribution in solidifying the social fabric of the empire, especially *vis-à-vis* waves of barbarian invasions, and converting and educating the populace in various parts of Europe. But even with the help of Christianity, or because of it, the Roman empire was split into two halves, much to the impoverishment of both the Latin and Byzantine cultural traditions. Europeans were also exposed to fierce power struggles between the ecclesiastical and political leaders. And, to make matters more serious, the disunited Western world was to witness the birth of Islam in the seventh century.

Islam: A New Religion and Empire

Although the history of Islam,[21] the life of Muhammad,[22] and its holy book, the Qur'ān,[23] merit discussion, we must confine ourselves here to some of the major issues involved in the relation between Islam as a religion and Islam as a civilization. On this problem, Reuben Smith rightly observes: "The Arab Muslims who came from the desert had precious little of what are thought of as the finer arts of civilization, but they *did* have something of the greatest moment: the Word of God as revealed through Muhammad; moreover they also had an outlook and an approach born of their background, social organization, values, and ideals, which put a stamp on Islamic civilization as it arose. The relationship of [Islam and] these original Muslim Arabs to the subsequent civilization as it grew is a problem of the greatest importance but not yet well understood."[24]

In viewing Islam there is a persistent—especially in the West—perception of it as a deviant offshoot of one prophetic tradition, traceable to the faith of Abraham. The real issue, I suspect, is the nature of the "spectacles" through which people (especially Westerners) look at the Islamic phenomenon, for in many instances they hardly look at Islam at all. Considering the gist of the Western religious-cultural-social-political synthesis, homologizing Near Eastern religions, Hellenistic cultural heritage, and Roman jurisprudence into a seamless unity, one can understand (which does not mean endorse) the strong motivation to view Judaism and Christianity as one continuous religion. From a "Christian" standpoint, Judaism prior to Jesus Christ was a *praeparatio evangelica*, to use the traditional Christian idiom. For Judaism, the holy book is the Hebrew Bible; the same, however, is accepted as the "Old" Testament by the Christian community. Thus, it is the prerogative of the Christian community to affirm as "Articles of Religion" (commonly referred to as the Thirty-Nine articles) that "the Old Testament is not contrary to the New: for both in the Old and New Testament everlasting life is offered to Mankind by Christ, who is the only Mediator between God and Man. . . ."[25] Yet the same Hebrew Bible has very different meanings for the Jewish community.

Understandably, from a Christian-centric perspective the continued existence of Judaism, independent of the European Christian "Judeo-Christian" religious tradition, became an embarrassment, both theologically and existentially. (Unfortunately, space does not allow us to discuss in this context the various phases of the horrendous treatment of Judaism in European history.) The Christian-inspired Western spectacle had two major built-in premises, namely, (i) salvation was a *fait accompli*, consummated by Jesus Christ, the only mediator between God and humankind and the fulfillment of all the prophecies mentioned in Jewish history, and (ii) the Christian church, the renewed covenanted community and the spiritual extension of Israel, was the only legitimate framework, potentially at least, for the unity of global humanity. Much to the amazement of many Westerners, these two premises—which to them appeared to be seemingly reasonable and rational—were effectively challenged by Islam.

Since the life of the founder of Islam, Muhammad, is well known, bare outlines will suffice here. Born ca. 571 into a poor Arabian family, his intense religious experiences convinced him to begin his prophetic career ca. 610. By chance he was invited to be the leader of the town of Medina, whereby he and his companions migrated there in A.D. 622; this event, called the *hejira*, marks the beginning of the official Islamic calendar. The humbler theocratic community which Muhammad established in Medina remained as the paradigm for the human community in the subsequent history of Islam. It is well to remember, as Frederick Denny reminds us, that "Islam came into being as a religion and a community inspired and regulated by a simultaneously emerging scripture. The Qur'ān, meaning 'recitation,' was orally revealed to . . . Muhammad by the Archangel Gabriel, according to Islamic belief, . . . [and] the Message itself claimed to be from a 'heavenly book' preserved in the presence of God."[26]

Historians tell us that both Judaism and Christianity were well known in Arabia during Muhammad's time, and there is every indication that Muhammad was familiar with Jewish and Christian lore. At least he claimed that the *ka'ba* (an old sanctuary situated in Mecca, believed to be the navel of the earth) had been originally consecrated by Abraham. In so doing, says von Grunebaum, "he gave greater depth to Arab historical consciousness, he prolonged the memories of his people to the day of Creation, and he gave them a spiritually significant tradition of holy history to supplement their ill-kept records of events of local importance."[27] Ironically, his frequent reference to many figures in the Jewish and Christian traditions gave the erroneous impression, especially to Westerners, that Islam could be understood as part of one religious tradition, which also embraces Judaism and Christianity, or worse yet, as a "misunderstanding" of the prophetic tradition. On this score, we agree with Gibb's well-known statement that "Islam is an autonomous expression of religious thought and experience, which must be viewed in and through itself and its own principles and standards."[28] If we affirm the autonomy of Islam as a self-authenticating and self-sufficient religion, we can fully understand the Muslim's conviction: "If God is one and His Message is also one and indivisible, surely mankind should be one community. And, particularly in view of the affirmation of his mission by followers of earlier religions, the Prophet hoped to unify the multiplicity of these religions into one single community, under his teachings and on his terms. . . ."[29]

It is a curious fact of history that many people accepted the Christian claim that Christ was the fulfillment of the Jewish Law and Prophets but reacted against Muhammad's claim to be the seal of the long line of prophets. (Here, we are not talking about one and the same religious tradition; what is involved is the Jewish, Christian, and Islamic religious perceptions, and we cannot judge one tradition by the standards of another.) What we learn from European history is, however, that many Christians interpreted the appearance of Muhammad as the coming of the false prophet as predicted in the Johannine apocalypse (Revelation 19:20).

The Western Image of Islam

One of the most remarkable facts about Islamic *religion* is that the small theocratic community in Medina (*umma muslima*) had within it the potential to spawn the great Islamic *civilization* which was to inherit the high civilization of the Byzantine and Sāsānian empires—more so than the Arabian desert tradition. As Reuben Smith succinctly points out, Islamic civilization of the tenth century was hardly of bedouin origin, and it was Arabic only in a linguistic sense:

> The *Arab* Muslims *conquered* all of the Sassanian Persian empire, and also the "fairest provinces" of the Byzantine, including many Byzantine intellectual centers, but *Muslims* and non-Muslims, only some of whose forefathers had come from the desert, built Islamic civilization. The Muslim capital of Damascus was built in former Byzantine territory, and the subsequent capital of Baghdad was only a few miles from the former Sassanian capital. . . . In the Islamic period [the word Arab] often refers to *inhabitants of the Fertile Crescent.* . . . Already by the ninth century the majority of *Muslims* had *not* come from *Arabia.*[30]

Indeed, during one century following the death of Muhammad in 632, Islamic civilization expanded not only to the eastern part of Byzantine and the former Sāsānian territories but also to Egypt and north Africa, as well as to the Iberian peninsula and some parts of Asia, attaining its widest geographical expansion between A.D. 717-732.

Like other great religious-cultural-social-political syntheses, the Islamic synthesis was many faceted. Western Christians, however, were initially preoccupied primarily by the religious aspect of Islam, particularly with the person of Muhammad and his claim to be *the* prophet. Persuaded as they were of the existence of only one religious tradition and having been taught that the salvation of humankind had already been enacted—"once and for all" (*einmalchkeit*)—by Jesus Christ, the Divine Word Incarnate, many Western Christians could not easily conceive the idea that someone other than Christ was the "Divine Word Inlibrate."[31] And, much as Jews at the time of the birth of Christianity could not accept the claim that Christ was the fulfillment of the "Law and the Prophets," it was now the Western Christians' turn to be baffled by the Islamic concept of the "perfect moral integrity or impeccability" (*'isma*) of Muhammad.[32] No less troubling was the claim that there were five great messengers in world history—Muhammad, Abraham, Moses, Jesus, and Noah—the most important being Muhammad as the seal of the prophets.

Confronted by Islam, Western Christians also had to reexamine their stance on history and community. In so doing, however, they were caught in a linguistic puzzle for Jews, Christians and Muslims used the same or similar terms with different meanings. Initially Christianity, following the Jewish view of God as the Lord of history, saw two kinds of history—(i) empirical history and (ii) the history of salvation (*Heilsgeschichte*) running through and behind empirical history. Then Christian apologists, who unlike the illiterate Galilean fishermen were highly educated in non-Christian philosophies, appropriated the Hellenistic term, *logos* ("speech," "reason," "rational faculty") and explained pre-Christian and non-Jewish religions in terms of the scattered seeds of *logos* (*logoi spermatikoi*), insisting that the history of salvation covered both the tradition of Moses, the patriarchs, and the prophets, and also the religious and philosophical traditions of Greece. The *logos* as teacher (*logos paidagōgos*) was active through these pre-Christian and non-Jewish traditions. And the same *logos* was incarnate in Christ, the second person of the Triune deity. Thus, Clement of Alexandria (c. 150-c. 215), for example, removed the difference between the history of divine salvation taught in the Hebrew scriptures and the history of non-Jewish religions and philosophies. In his view, according to Ernst Benz, "the history of salvation, soteriology, was not separated from the general history of mankind; *Heilsgeschichte* was not a disconnected improvisation inserted into universal history but, rather, included and covered the whole human development."[33]

The gradual consolidation of Christian soteriology was strengthened further by Emperor Theodosius's advocacy of Trinitarian orthodoxy in 380. Many Christians affirmed the "frozen," exclusivistic view of salvation. This held that all pre-Christian religions, including Judaism prior to Christ, were fulfilled by Christ, the *logos* incarnate, whereby Christ alone is the savior not only of those "who received him, who believed in his name," as the Johannine Gospel (1:12) states, but of all others, including those yet to be born, in every corner of the earth—for perpetuity. No wonder Western Christians were not inclined to accept Muhammad as the messenger of the new gospel who would fulfill all previous prophecies and revelations, including those of Christianity. Thus, he was often classified by Western Christians as a false prophet.

**   *   *   *   *

The soteriology of Western Christianity is grounded in the simple logic that Christ, the divine-human savior, is said to have handpicked Peter to become the cornerstone of the Christian community, and because Peter was martyred in Rome, his successors as bishops of Rome were to serve as Christ's vicar on earth. Moreover, only the Christian church, even though it is humanly established and organized, is mystically animated as the holy and universal community, potentially anyway, for every human being. Hence the affirmation: "*credo . . . unam sanctam catholicam ecclesiam.*" Such a self-understanding of the Christian church was bound to come in conflict with the Islamic understanding of humanity and its own community. There is some evidence that at first Muhammad thought he was bringing to the Arabs the same message which the Jews had received from Moses and the Christians from Jesus; there is even the recognition of three separate communities—Jews, Christians, and Muslims.[34] But later the term *Umma* and the term "the People of the Book" came to be used more frequently. Although the Qur'ān recognizes "in some fashion the validity of the Jewish and the Christian communities," Rahman reminds us, "still, the Muslim community remains the 'ideal' or 'best' community. . . .[35] Eventually, Islam divided the world into two spheres—(i) the *dār al-Islām*, the regions under the control of Islam, and (ii) *dār al-Harb*, the regions not subjected to it, and it came to be believed that "between this 'area of warfare' and the Muslim-dominated part of the world there can be no peace."[36]

After Muhammad's death, the Islamic community created the institution of the Caliphate to guide and administer—but not religiously—the *Umma*, so that it would faithfully observe the *Sharia* (the holy law of Islam). The caliph was, in theory at least, the symbol of the unity of the Islamic community. The first caliphate, the Umayyad dynasty (A.D. 661-750) with its capital in Damascus, emulated the ethos (especially the relationship between piety and political rule), culture, and bureaucratic structure of the Byzantine empire. Aided by the Syrian army, the Umayyad dynasty also greatly expanded the Islamic community from the Iberian peninsula in the West to Sind in the East, conquering territories as far north as Khwarezum, Samakand, and Fergena.   It was the Umayyad which ignored the practice of election, that presumably would make the caliph "first among equals" of his peers and introduced the principle of hereditary succession. The Umayyad's ascendancy was achieved, however, at the expense of the creation of a group called the *Shi'a* ("Separate party" or followers of the fourth caliph, Alī, who was the rival of the Umayyad's ruler). This group continued to acknowledge only Alī's descendants as legitimate rulers or *imams* of Islam.   When the Umayyad dynasty was defeated by the second caliphate, the Abbāsid, one of the Umayyad's members escaped assassination and went to Spain where he became the *emir* (prince) of the Iberian Islamic community.

The Abbāsid dynasty (A.D. 750-1258), with its capital in Baghdad in the heartland of the former Sāsānian kingdom, rejected the Umayyad's policy of making overtures toward the Mediterranean world and focused its attention on eastern development. With strong support from the faithful in Persia and Transoxania, the Abbāsid dynasty admired and preserved the legacy of the Sāsānian empire. Although the Arab language continued to be used under the Abbāsid dynasty, the membership of the *Umma* were now largely Muslim believers who were not necessarily Arabs by nationality. The Abbāsid rule also introduced the service of non-Muslims such as the Berbers and Turks (who became Muslims). Thus, the Islamic community under the Abbāsid dynasty became increasingly more like another Oriental theocracy, and as Hitti points out, "gradually Persian titles, Persian wines and wives, Persian mistresses, Persian songs, as well as Persian ideas and thoughts, won the day."[37]

*   *   *   *   *

At any rate, what Western Christians encountered after Muhammad's death was not only the energetic, growing religion of Islam, but a highly complex Islamic civilization, inspired by the Sāsānian and Byzantine traditions. The Islamic community wisely preserved such cultural centers as Nisibis, Edessa, and Alexandria. Also, the Abbāsid rulers were especially keen on sponsoring translations of important works from other languages into Arabic. According to Kraemer: "The first stage was the translation into Arabic of works on Greek philosophy and science from Syriac (or Aramaic), because before the advent of Islam the Eastern-Syrian Nestorians and the Western-Syrian Monophysites had absorbed the Hellenistic heritage by translation into Aramaic. . . . The translators were nearly all Christians, who became the real culture transmitters and so enabled scholarly-minded 'Muslims' to deploy their gifts, using as their basis and material the legacy of Oriental-Greek learning and thought..."[38] As might be expected, Islamic civilization made significant contributions to Europe, then far from being civilized, especially through the Islamic community in Spain (called Al-Andalus by the Muslims). Shortly after the Muslims' landing in the Iberian peninsula in A.D. 711, they began to control a major portion of Spain. Although Spanish Muslims continued to receive cultural influence from the Middle East, they lived as an independent political unit within the Islamic community, as exemplified by the existence of the caliphate (912-1031) in Cordova. Clearly Muslims had very advanced knowledge of trade, philosophy, science, literature and the arts, and their libraries and universities in Spain, especially in such centers as Al Hakam, Toledo, and Cordova, attracted a number of Christian and Jewish scholars from various parts of Europe. No doubt Djait is right in stating: "Islam was at once a military force threatening Europe and an economic sphere sharing its dynamism, just as later it would be an ideological enemy and a philosophical model. In a word, Europe's emergence into history took place . . . through the mediation of Islam: in the beginning by means of a defensive recoil, afterward by an offensive explosion."[39]

The Islamic Community Between Europe and Asia

In medieval history west of India, there were three autonomous political and cultural units—the Islamic community, Byzantine Christendom, and Latin Christendom—each with different rhythms of rise and decline. As von Grunebaum notes: "These units represent compact blocs only when set against one another. . . . each is ruled by a central government, and political theory never ceases to uphold the *fiction of unity* when actually the territory of each of the three power blocs has been divided among . . . [an] increasing number of princes. . . . *This fiction of unity* reflects a powerful sentiment of cultural oneness within the area of each bloc and, to a great extent, retards and obscures its decomposition."[40]   True to von Grunebaum's thesis, the Islamic community during the tenth century had three contending caliphs, one each in Baghdad, in Cairo and in Spain, while in the eleventh century the Latin West had three competing popes and the Byzantine bloc was divided into three rival factions, each with its own emperor. The fact that there were three autonomous communities (each one divided into small factions) suggests the difficulty of sorting out facts and claims.

One of the most intriguing aspects of medieval Europe's relation to Islam was its apparent double dealings. Europe was most eager to receive cultural, philosophical, and religious contributions from Iberian Muslims, yet almost simultaneously its Crusaders were fighting against Middle Eastern Muslims. The Crusades were a series of military campaigns by the West European Christian princes from 1096 to 1291 for the purpose of recovering the Holy Land from Muslim rule. As far as we can ascertain, the Crusades—despite the heavy loss of European lives—made little, if any, dent in the Islamic community. Certainly these campaigns, fought with very mixed motives, probably bolstered the fictional unity of the Latin West by bringing papal and political leaders in Europe a little closer, but the Crusades also caused further alienation. Above all the Crusades left four major and far-reaching "negative" legacies to subsequent history.

First, by pushing the dimension of the military conflict with the Islamic community to the forefront, the Crusades erased from the memories of Western Christians their great philosophical, religious and cultural indebtedness to Muslims, especially to those in Spain, Sicily, and Provence. Numerically speaking, the Muslim elements were negligible in Europe, and some Jews and Christians were included among the ranks of Muslim intelligentsia in the Islamic community. Nevertheless it was still remarkable that through the contact with the relatively small Muslim groups, Europe learned the rich heritages of Hellenistic, Persian (and Indian to a small extent), and Islamic traditions in philosophy, mysticism, alchemy, medicine, chemistry, mathematics, optics, astronomy, musical theory, law, etc. The great Muslim philosopher Averroes (A.D. 1126-1198) of Cordova, Spain, was so influential among the Jews that they later even formed an Averroist school of thought, promoted by the Cordova-born Jewish philosopher Maimonides (A.D. 1135-1204) (who incidentally wrote many of his works in Arabic). Moreover, al-Ghazzālī, another famous Muslim theologian, as well as Averroes, influenced Thomas Aquinas (A.D. c. 1225-1274). Thomas and his Dominican teacher, Albertus Magnus (c. 1200-1280), read "Arab" commentaries on Aristotle in Latin translations. We are told that "[Thomas] was conversant with Avicenna (Ibn Sīnā, d. 1037), the greatest philosopher and scholar of Oriental Islam, the Jewish Aristoteleans Maimonides and Ibn Gabirol, ... the second of whom had strong Neo-Platonist leanings . . . [and] the first 'Arab' philosopher in Occidental Islam, Ibn Bajja, in Latin called Avempace (d. 1138), to mention only a few."[41] According to some scholars, even the *Divine Comedy* of Dante (1265-1321) was greatly influenced by the Islamic literary tradition. Yet, the Crusades made it difficult for Europeans to acknowledge these important contributions.

Second, though the Crusades were in a strict sense not "religious" wars because of their mixed motives, they nevertheless left a negative religious impact on the psyche of Europeans, that augmented a belligerent attitude toward Islam. The astonishing fact is that very few European Christians bothered to know the main tenets of Islamic religion. They were only sure that Christianity as they knew it had the final truth.

This might account for Western Christians' indifference toward as well as their repudiation of the sacred book of Islam, the Qur'ān:

> The first Latin translation of the [Qur'ān] was prepared by Petrus Venerabilis, Abbot of Cluny, in 1144, fifty years after Pope Urban II proclaimed the first crusade and five hundred years after [the compilation of] the definitive edition of the [Qur'ān]; however, Bernard of Clairvaux opposed very bitterly this Latin translation. The next publication of the same Latin version . . . came out in 1542/43, four hundred years later; but . . . the Protestant authorities in Basel . . . put the editor and the printer in jail. . . . After another hundred years of silence, in 1612, a new Latin version of the [Qur'ān] was edited by Ludovico Maracci in Rome, together with a Roman Catholic refutation of the doctrines of Mohammed.[42]

It might be instructive to compare the attitude of medieval European Christians toward Islam with the humble attitude of Gamaliel toward the new Christian community. At that time, Gamaliel, the religious person *par excellence*, spoke simply: "If this plan or this undertaking [referring to the infant Christianity] is of men, it will fail; but if it is of God, you will not be able to overthrow them" (Acts 5:38-39).

The medieval European Christian attitude toward Islam undoubtedly reflected the ethos of the official church, which had forgotten the earlier Christian emphasis on faith and the free operation of the divine spirit in favor of the claim of authority. And once this self-understanding of the earthly church is affirmed and the ecclesiastical authority proclaims another religion to be a mortal enemy, distorted perceptions of the other arise. As Norman Daniel astutely observes: "Apparently, under the pressure of their sense of danger, whether real or imagined, a deformed image of their enemy's beliefs takes shape in man's minds. By misapprehension and misrepresentation an idea of the beliefs and practices of one society can pass into the accepted myths of another society in a form so distorted that its relation to the original facts is sometimes barely

discernible. Doctrines that are the expression of the spiritual outlook of an enemy are modified—and in good faith—to suit the interpretation."[43]   Indeed, the medieval European Christians' attitude toward Islam was a text-book case.

Third, was the manner in which, following the Crusades, European Christians' image of Islamic religion and culture became the
yardstick for Europeans' evaluations of all other non-Western cultures. As far as we know, ancient contacts between Europe and
China, or Europe and India, were not always fraternal in nature,
but neither were the East-West relationships dominated by mutual
bigotry and condescension. We know, for example, that, following
Alexander's Indian campaign, the Greco-Bactrian kingdoms acted
as cultural and trade brokers between India and Europe. One of
the Greek kings in Panjāb, Menander (or Milinda), studied under
the philosopher-monk, Nāgasena, and was reputed to have become
a Buddhist himself.[44]   Meanwhile, the overland routes between
Europe and China served as channels for the exchange of goods,
cultures, and ideas. Needham tells us that "what knowledge the
ancient peoples of the Mediterranean basin had of China . . . concerned mostly silk and the trade in silk, and the geographical
knowledge which arose directly out of this. But it is worth noticing
that some rumours of Confucianism seem to have reached Europe
as early as the 2nd century. . . ."[45] We also know there was a sufficient amount of Indian influence on such European Christian leg-
end-lore as "St. Eustace," "St. Christopher," and "Satan as tempter
in the savior's form," while at the same time there is evidence of
Christian influence on Buddhism and later Krishnaism.[46]

The early Christian community, surrounded by non-Christian
people, was nevertheless not known for a reprehensive attitude to
non-Christians. The early Christians stuck together, convinced
that divine grace was operative within their community, which to
them was *in* the world but not *of* the world. Significantly, the
Gospel of Luke (Chapter 24:13-31) portrays the prototype of the
Christian community in the walking of two Christian disciples on
the road to Emmaus, "talking with each other about all these things
that had happened." They felt so strongly about what they had

heard and seen that they shared their experience with a total "stranger" on the road who turned out to be Christ himself. Even after Christianity became the official religion some European Christians had enough intellectual modesty to receive the heritage of antiquity from Muslim intellectuals, and even in the midst of fighting, some Europeans had respect and admiration for the courage of Muslim soldiers. But gradually after the Crusades, Europeans transferred the derogatory images of Islam and Muslims to all other non-Christians.

Fourth, such an uninformed hostile and condescending attitude of Western Christendom was destined to leave gloomy, dark shadows on such later phenomena as colonialism, Christian world mission, and the expansion of modern Western civilization to the entire non-Western world. Suffice it to conclude by citing the most extraordinary dogmatic statement, passed at the Council of Florence in 1438-45, *extra ecclesiam nulla salus* ("outside the church there is no salvation"), which came to be deeply ingrained in the hearts of many Europeans.

*   *   *   *   *

While the fictional unity of the Islamic community was visibly broken by the three contending caliphs in the tenth century, the interracial Islamic community continued to expand, although it was now ruled by many independent local governments. Notwithstanding the extravagant claims to universality of Latin and Byzantine Christendom, Marshall Hodgson was no doubt right in stating that at the time of the Crusades, the Islamic community "was certainly the most widely spread and influential society on the globe."[47] The Islamic community was simultaneously expanding in many directions—Africa, Central Asia, and South Asia. No one is certain when Islam first reached China, but we can follow the arrival of the Muslims both by means of the ocean route and the overland route. At any rate, according to Latourette, "in 758 Arabs and Persians were sufficiently strong in Canton to loot the city. . . ."[48] In the course of time, much as both Latin and Byzantine

Christendom converted barbarians in their border areas, Islam, too, converted the Seljūk Turks and other tribal groups, adding them to the ever-growing Islamic community.

To the Islamic community, the sacking of Baghdad by the Mongols in 1258 was far more frightening and devastating than the Crusades. Soon, Ghengis Khan's grandson established the Mongol kingdom of Persia. Eventually, however, a large segment of Mongols became Muslims. The Mongols had driven out the Ottoman Turks from their home in Central Asia, hence the Ottomans occupied much of Anatolia by the fourteenth century. They were defeated by the Tartar leader, Tamerlane, but soon recovered, capturing the Byzantine capital, Constantinople, in 1453. Meanwhile, the fall of Granada to Christian forces in 1492 signified the end of the Muslims foothold in Europe. Yet Islam was a powerful fixture, with which both Europe and Asia had to reckon.

We shall now see how this impasse was broken by the aggressive initiatives of Europeans.

Notes

1 J.M. Kitagawa, "East and West--A Dialogue," *Perspectives* (South Bend, Indiana: Notre Dame University Press), VI, (January-February 1961), 19.

2 H.J. Muller, *The Use of the Past: Profiles of Former Societies* (New York: The New American Library of World Literature, Inc., 1952), 53-54.

3 C.W. Bishop, "The Beginning of Civilization in Eastern Asia," *The Beginnings of Civilization in the Orient*, Supplement to the *Journal of the American Oriental Society*, No. 4 (December 1939), 46.

4 Quoted in J. Finegan, *The Archaeology of World Religions* (Princeton: Princeton University Press, 1952), 96.

5 Recorded in his famous Rock Edict 12, cited in Amulyachandra Sen, *Aśoka's Edicts* (Calcutta: The Indian Publicity Society, 1956), 94.

6 J. Muilenburg, "The Ethics of the Prophet," in Anshen, *Moral Principles of Action*, 530.

7 *Ibid.*, 536; my italics.

8 D.R. Cartlidge and D.L. Dungan, *Documents for the Study of the Gospels* (Philadelphia: Fortress Press, 1980), 17-18.

9 *Ibid.*, 15.

10 A.L. Basham, *The Wonder That Was India* (New York: Grove Press, 1954), 59.

11 *Ibid.*, 274.

12 See Needham, *Science and Civilization in China*, Volume 1, especially Chapter 7, "Conditions of Travel of Scientific Ideas and Techniques between China and Europe," 150-206.

13 F. Teggart, *Rome and China: A Study of Correlations in Historical Events* (Berkeley: University of California Press, 1939), vii.

14 Thomas Hopkins, *The Hindu Religious Tradition* (Encino: Dickenson, 1971), 108.

15 Basham, *The Wonder*, 228.

16 Winston King, "Religion," in Eliade, *The Encyclopedia of Religion*, XII, 282 and 285.

17 J.M. Kitagawa, *On Understanding Japanese Religion* (Princeton: Princeton University Press, 1987), 48-49.

18 See E.G. Hinson, "Irenaeus," *The Encyclopedia of Religion* (New York: Macmillan, 1987), VII, 280-283.

19 Peter Brown, *Augustine of Hippo* (Berkeley: University of California Press, 1967), 214.

20 Talcott Parsons, "Christianity," *The International Encyclopedia of the Social Sciences* (New York: Macmillan, 1968), II, 432.

21 See Marshall G.S. Hodgson, *The Venture of Islam*, ed. by R.W. Smith (3 vols.; Chicago: The University of Chicago Press, 1974).

22 See Annemarie Schimmel, *And Muhammad is His Messenger* (Chapel Hill: The University of North Carolina Press, 1985).

23 See Fazlur Rahman, *Major Themes of the Qu'rān* (Minneapolis: Bibliotheca Islamica, 1980).

24 Reuben W. Smith, ed., *Islamic Civilization in the Middle East* (Chicago: The University of Chicago--Committee on Near Eastern Studies, 1965), 10.

25 Cited from *The Book of Common Prayer* (New York: The Church Hymnal Corporation, 1977), 869.

26 F.M. Denny and R.L. Taylor, eds., *The Holy Book in Comparative Perspective* (Columbia: University of South Carolina Press, 1985), 84.

27 G.E. von Grunebaum, *Medieval Islam* (Chicago: The University of Chicago Press, 1946), 3.

28 H.A.R. Gibb, *Mohammedanism: An Historical Survey* (London: Oxford University Press, 1953), 6.

29 Rahman, *Major Themes*, 138.

30 Smith, *Islamic Civilization*, 9.

31 Schimmel, *And Muhammad is His Messenger*, 24. She notes that this expression came from Harri Wolfson.

32 *Ibid.*, 56.

33 Ernst Benz, "The Theological Meaning of the History of Religions," *The Journal of Religion*, XLI:1 (January 1961), 5.

34 Rahman, *Major Themes*, 144.

35 *Ibid.*, 145.

36 Grunebaum, *Medieval Islam*, 9.

37 P.K. Hitti, *The Arabs—A Short History* (Princeton: Princeton University Press, 1949), 39.

38 Kraemer, *World Cultures and World Religions*, 38-39.

39 H. Djait, *Europe and Islam* (Berkeley: University of California Press, 1985), 109.

40 Grunebaum, *Medieval Islam*, 1; my italics.

41 Kraemer, *World Cultures*, 49.

42 Benz, "The Theological Meaning," 7.

43 N. Daniel, *Islam and the West—The Making of an Image* (Edinburgh: University Press, 1960), 2.

44 Basham, *The Wonder*, 59.

45 Needham, *Science and Civilization*, I, 157.

46   On this intriguing subject, see Richard Garbe, *India and Christendom: The Historical Connections Between Their Religions* (La Salle: The Open Court, 1959).

47   Hodgson, *The Venture of Islam*, II, 3.

48   K.S. Latourette, *The Chinese: Their History and Culture* (New York: Macmillan, 1934), I, 204.

Chapter Three

Revolution and Tradition

Before Columbus and Vasco da Gama

Earlier we talked about the three layers of the mental universe of Asians. At the bottom is the historical "world of meaning"—living close to the world of nature, considering the cosmos as a gigantic living community of beings that includes, of course, non-human beings as well. These basic cosmological themes are shared widely throughout Asia, although they are arranged differently by various cultural, religious, ethnic and linguistic groups. I borrowed William S. Haas's expression, "juxtaposition," to describe the traditional Asian pattern of affirming the autonomy of diverse cultural and religious traditions. According to this relative principle, each group lives in a self-authenticating wholeness. Hence, Easterners and Westerners do not divide human life and experience in the same way. If one uses Western categories—religion, culture, aesthetics, and ethics, etc.—to describe the Easterners' understanding, one might say the autonomous worlds of meaning of different groups amount to a religious-cultural-social-political synthesis. Characteristic of such a synthesis is a seamless circularity taken for granted as self-evidently true. These syntheses are the civilizations of India, China, Southeast Asia, Korea, Japan, Islam, etc.

In The Western tradition, on the other hand, fused its different elements—Near Eastern religious traditions, the Hellenistic intellectual heritage, and Roman jurisprudence (which in itself embodied the convergence of different social and political features)—into a unified European civilization that refused to admit the autonomy of its constituent parts. In this respect, Christianity played a precarious role in Europe in that its original eschatological and supramundane orientations yielded to a this-worldly outlook, especially after Constantine the Great made it an official religion of the empire in the early fourth century. It is interesting to note that, reflecting the Western impulse for a homology of diverse elements, Christianity indulged in its own formulae for merging, i.e., the notion of the history of salvation (*Heilsgeschichte*) which it inherited from the Hebrew religious tradition and the concept of *logos* ("speech," "reason," "rational faculty") which it appropriated from Hellenism. Thus Christianity came to advance an apologetic theology that said in effect that diverse religions, cultures, and philosophies everywhere prior to the Christ-event had contained scattered seeds of divine *logos* (*logoi spermatikoi*). These traditions were, though unconsciously, the instruments of the *logos* as teacher (*logos Paidagōgos*) who was born as the *logos*-incarnate in Jesus Christ. Christianity also constructed an elaborate ecclesiology by piecing together myths, legends, pious hopes, and political realities. Thus, joining Biblical references, the faith of Peter as the foundation of Christianity, and the legends of his martyrdom in Rome, Western Christianity now claimed that the bishops of Rome were successors to Peter as Christ's vicar on earth. And, as stated in the last chapter, the logical conclusion of such trends in Christianity was the dogmatic assertion: *extra ecclesiam nulla salus* ("outside the church there is no salvation"). Such extravagant claims provided the cosmic legitimation needed by the Western religious-cultural-social-political synthesis.

With this kind of orientation many Westerners, especially Western Christians, had difficulties swallowing the birth of another religion of salvation such as that initiated by Muhammad in seventh-century Arabia. Certainly Muhammad's claim that he was the seal of the prophets, fulfilling all previous revelations including those of Christianity, did not sit well with Western Christians who were told that salvation already had been accomplished by Jesus Christ. Therefore many Western Christians condemned Muhammad as a false prophet and dubbed Islam as counterfeit religion based on a misunderstanding of Judaism and Christianity (interpreted by the

Western Christian church, of course). Significantly, Islam generated its own form of religious-cultural-social-political synthesis, one that inherited the high civilizations of the Byzantine and Sāsānian traditions, both of them heirs to Hellenistic-Persian antiquity. Ironically, Europe depended on the religious and cultural contributions of European Muslims, while fighting militarily against Middle Eastern Muslims in the Crusades.

Islamic religion, civilization, and community occupied a strategic geographical area, situated between the Western and Eastern parts of Eurasia and along the corridor to Africa. It is not an exaggeration to say that the Islamic community served for centuries as a buffer zone, separating Europe and Asia. Thus, although there were very limited and sporadic cultural and commercial contacts between Europeans and Asians, between the eighth and the fifteenth centuries, the West and the East went along, more or less uninformed of what was happening to the other. Islam was seen from the perspectives of Europe and Asia as an impenetrable obstacle. As a result, Muslims saw themselves as destined to serve both as commercial and cultural brokers and as agents for the eternal salvation of the entire world.

Meanwhile, Islam was not idle in Africa, the Caucasus, the Middle Volga area, and South and Southeast Asia. Islam was particularly successful in southern Asia. Arab Muslim traders were active in coastal towns around the Indian ocean as early as the eighth century. By the tenth century, there were Muslim settlements in the Deccan. From the thirteenth to the sixteenth centuries much of North India was already ruled by a series of Muslim dynasties, and most of India was then claimed by the Muslim Mughal dynasty (1526-1761). In comparison with India, Islamic expansion was slower and less spectacular in Southeast Asia. There is, however, evidence that Muslim traders were settled in coastal cities of Sumatra, the Malay peninsula, Borneo and Java around the eleventh century. There "the territories of the Islamic commonwealth in Southeast Asia were so vast that the process of their creation has been called the second expansion of Islam, alluding to the original expansion from Arabia into North Africa and the Fertile Crescent."[1] Needless to say, Islamization greatly altered the faces of South and Southeast Asia.

Other important changes in the medieval period also had cross-national implications. In 635, Syrian Nestorians (followers of the fifth century bishop of Constantinople, Nestorius, who held that Christ had two separate persons, divine and human) sent a missionary to China, then known for its liberal policy toward other religions. Evidently, Nestorianism found followers among the Chinese and different border tribes, including the Mongols. A few centuries later, during the Mongol Yüan dynasty (A.D. 1276-1368), the emperors of China were descendants of none other than Genghis Khan (1162-1227), who had united the tribes of the steppe and hoped to conquer other parts of the world. A Mongol army sacked the Islamic capital of Baghdad in 1258, toppling the Abbāsid caliphate. In addition, the first ruler of the Mongol khannate of Persia was Hulagu, the grandson of Genghis.

With the Mongol dominance over the trade routes between China and Persia, some European merchants, especially those from Venice and Genoa, took advantage of the new situation for commercial profit. Moreover, some friars were sent to Mongolia for political and diplomatic errands. A Franciscan, John of Plano Carpini (who went to see the great Mongol khan in A.D. 1245-47), was followed by another Franciscan, William of Rubruck, who visited Mongolia in 1253-55.[2] Another grandson of Genghis, Khubilai Khan (r. 1260-1294), became the emperor of all China. Khubilai befriended a Venetian traveller, Marco Polo, who spent two decades in his court as his confidential advisor. According to René Grousset: "The life of the Nestorian communities in China under Khubilai is well known through the story of the patriarch Mar Yabalaha and Rabban Sauma. Rabban Sauma (1225-1294) and Rabban Marcos were two Nestorian monks, the former born near Peking, the latter in . . . Suiyüan, who in 1275 or 1276 left China to make a pilgrimage to Jerusalem. . . . The khan of Persia . . . caused Marcos to be elected to the Nestorian patriarchal throne. . . ."[3] It is also important to note that Sauma became the Persian ambassador in 1287 and was sent to Europe to form an alliance between the

Crusaders and the Mongols against the Muslims. In Paris he talked with King Philip and was cordially received in Rome by Pope Nicholas IV. Nothing came of this negotiation, however, due to the indecisiveness on the part of Europe. (Later, the Mongol khanate of Persia embraced Islam.)

In 1294, John of Montecorvino, the first friar to reach China proper, arrived by way of India at the Chinese capital. He is reputed to have baptized approximately six thousand converts. In 1342, John of Marigolli, a papal delegate, arrived in China with ambitious plans for the future of the Chinese church. But shortly afterwards, the Mongol regime fell, and nothing more was heard of the Christian community in China for two centuries.

On the European side too, a series of changes with far-reaching implications began to take place. During the twelfth and the thirteenth centuries, the tightly organized, ecclesiastically controlled medieval synthesis of religion-culture-society-political order gave way to the development of towns, trade, industry, and a middle class. The European intellectual vista was greatly stretched by both the impact of Muslim learning and the recovery of Antiquity through the growth of Scholastic theology and philosophy. The new intellectual climate in Europe anticipated the phenomenal rise of medieval universities[4] and the Renaissance initiated by Italian humanists in the fourteenth century. Many Europeans began to question the medieval paradigm of three divinely-ordained institutions—*Sacerdotium* ("church"), *Imperium* ("state"), and *Studium* ("university")—described in the famous thirteenth century document, *The Chronicles of Jordanus Teutonicus*.[5] Although Europe did not repudiate Christianity per se, many Europeans after the Renaissance rejected the medieval notion that the church was the guardian of civilization. They began to find fulfillment of human life in secular, especially political, life. The spirit of the new European synthesis, which had its share of racism and narcissism, became a sort of pseudo-religion of secularized salvation.

Due to its stress on humanism, the Renaissance tended to be anti-clerical. When the spirit of the Renaissance crossed the mountains to northern Europe, however, it inspired various Protestant Reformations. The military threat of Suleyman I (d. 1566), sultan of the Ottoman Empire, to Vienna in 1532 compelled the anti-Protestant Emperor Charles V of the Holy Roman Empire to acknowledge *de facto* the Lutheran Reformation in Germany. Martin Luther (1483-1546) and many other reformers dared to defy Rome (*Sacerdotium*) for the truth of Christianity which they had learned in the universities (*Studium*). Therefore, after the Reformation, Rome rejected the truth claims of the university (*Studium*) in favor of the papacy's exclusive monopoly over the *Magisterium* ("teaching office"). Yet although the reformers repudiated papal sacerdotalism, they were not critical of the statement: *extra ecclesiam nulla salus*. In fact, they affirmed the same principle for their reformed churches.

Asia prior to Vasco da Gama and Columbus (during the fourteenth and fifteenth centuries), lacked the aggressive energy in commercial, political, cultural, religious, and scientific matters which was so clearly evident in the West in the same period. The remarkable events which occurred in Asia were of a different character. For example, in India the merging of Hinduism and Islam resulted in the birth of a third tradition, called Sikhism, advocated by Kabīr (c. 1440-1518) and Guru Nānak (1469-1539). (One cannot help but wonder how the originally irenic spirit of Sikhism came to produce the militant, exclusive ethos of the Sikhs in the twentieth century.) In some ways more astonishing than the birth of Sikhism was the eclecticism of the great Mughal emperor Akbar (r. 1556-1606) who established the Hall of Worship, open to the adherents of Islam, Hinduism, Zoroastrianism, and Christianity. Although he remained a Muslim officially, he married a Hindu woman and allowed Hindu worship in the palace. From 1582 onward he espoused his own eclectic faith, which he called the Divine Faith. A thoroughgoing reformer, Akbar also tried to eliminate such traditional Hindu customs as *sātī* (cremation of the widow), excessive dowries, and slavery. In all this, he was probably ahead of his time. His eclectic religious faith did not survive him, primarily because it lacked organizational structure. In fact, after his death, Akbar's activities had no lasting influence either in India or in the Islamic world.

After the fall of the Mongol Yüan dynasty in China in 1368, the native Chinese dynasty of the Ming (1368-1644) was in a better position to develop a synthesis of the Confucian, Taoist, and Buddhist traditions as well as of the Neo-Confucianism (itself an eclectic system) of the Sung period (960-1279), the internationalistic legacy of the Yüan period, and the newly awakened political and cultural nationalism. Some of the early Ming monarchs, especially the Hung-wu Emperor (r. 1368-1399) and the Yung-lo Emperor (r. 1403-1425) were unusually able and effective leaders who skillfully used the Ming tributary system to dominate East Asia. Yung-lo hand-picked the eunuch-admiral Cheng Ho (of non-Han descent, a Muslim from Yunnan, which was incorporated as a part of China proper by the Ming rule) who conducted seven maritime missions and incorporated some Southeast Asian nations as tributaries to China. But the Ming's dependency on the civil service examination system as the only access to official positions developed a tight, inflexible social and cultural system. And the unwise abuse of the tributary system may have flattered China's exaggerated view of its cultural and political importance, eventually resulting in a heavy financial drain on the government. To make matters worse, the Ming monarchs after the mid-fifteenth century were consistently second-rate, particularly the Wan-li Emperor who was notorious for the indifference and lack of ability during his 48 years (1572-1620) of his reign.

By the middle ages Japan, despite its size, could no longer be ignored in East Asia. Earlier Japan had synthesized its own indigenous, archaic, cosmic tradition (which became the basis for the native religion called Shinto, "the *kami* way") with Chinese traditions (Confucianism, Taoism, and Yin-Yang system) and Buddhism under the authority of the emperor, who functioned simultaneously as the chief priest of the nation, the sacred king, and the living *kami* (by virtue of his or her solar ancestry). During the Heian period (ninth to the twelfth centuries) Japan indigenized foreign elements and began to develop its own cultural forms. Then during the Kamakura period (thirteenth and early fourteenth centuries), Japan experienced a heightened religious awakening, especially among Buddhists but also among Shinto adherents. During this period, Japan was ruled by its first feudal regime (*bakufu* or *shōgunate*), the warrior government under the generalissimo (*shōgun*). In 1274 and again in 1281, Chinese forces under Khubilai Khan attempted to invade Japan but were rebuffed by a storm which the Japanese called "the divine wind." In 1338, the Ashikaga feudal regime began its rule of Japan. But the breakdown of the social and political fabric soon became evident, the result of incessant warfare over the years (1467-1477) known as the Ōnin War. Afterwards, many warriors fought among themselves until the unification of Japan was achieved by three strongmen, Oda Nobunaga (1534-1582), Toyotomi Hideyoshi (1536-1598), and Tokugawa Iyeyasu (1542-1616).

To summarize, by the end of the fifteenth century the world had three main actors, as it were—(i) the West, enthusiastically pursuing its course toward unity and synthesis, actively and ambitiously looking for commercial and other outside contacts confident in its status as the best and only true civilization; (ii) the East, affirming the autonomy of various religious-cultural-social-political syntheses, inclined to complacency and dormancy; and (iii) the world of Islam, consciously occupying a strategic geographical position, expanding rapidly into many directions, but preoccupied with internal problems.

Westernization of the East

The impact of the West introduced Asia to its Western civilization—characterized earlier as a *de facto* pseudo-religion of secularized salvation—and re-interpreted Eastern cultural and religious traditions from a Western perspective. One must bear in mind the historical differences between the earlier phase in the sixteenth and seventeenth centuries led by the Iberian kingdoms, Portugal and Spain, and the later phase in the eighteenth and nineteenth centuries which included many other European nations, as well as the United States. In addition, the second phase is characterized by the Christian world mission, and Western non-religious, humanistic, scientific, and technological influences are not easily distinguished. We must avoid the temptation to moralize about past events. Thus, although we cannot rationally explain why, for a variety of reasons Asia "stopped developing politically, economically, and socially around 1400, just about the time that the Western nations started on a period of extraordinary growth with the exploration and colonial expansion, the Renaissance, the Reformation, the English, French, and American revolutions, and the Industrial Revolution."[6] Nor can we explain why the Islamic community, which despite the temporary disruption by Timur (Timur Lang or Tamerlanc, d. 1405) was expanding rapidly in Africa and Asia during the fifteenth century, but was not strong enough to offset the advance of the West. It may be that Muslim communities in Anatolia, Egypt, the Iberian peninsula, the Middle East, India, etc. were preoccupied with their own internal problems, and lacked the cooperation needed for such a show of force. (This may account for the tragic fall of lonely Granada, the last Muslim hold in Spain.)

We must also think more "relationally" in dealing with significant events. We may be accustomed to viewing life compartmentally, hence we seek a primarily religious explanation for what we call "religious" events and look for political factors involved in political events. Yet, political and religious events may be very closely related, a possibility that modern Western thought often overlooks.

* * * * *

During the rise of the West, the Iberian peninsula was the only part of Europe which was under direct Muslim domination. During the hundreds of years of the Christian-Muslim power struggle, many qualities of the Islamic community, especially its this-worldly orientation, influenced Iberian Christians. As an effective this-worldly religion, Christianity was no match for Islam, which used its other-worldly objective to bolster the importance of its this-worldly community. On this intricate dialectic, von Grunebaum writes:

(1) Islam sets for life an otherworldly goal. . . . Accordingly, the aims of heathen ambition, such as wealth, power, fame, remain acceptable aspirations only inasmuch as they are integrated in the organizational structure of the new life. (2) By making the individual responsible for his fate in the next world, the new faith completed . . . the process of legal and moral individuation. . . . (3) By accepting the indispensability of the community to the fulfillment of some of the basic obligations of the individual, Islam stressed the necessity of . . . the political community coextensive with the area of the faith—and therefore ultimately destined to dominate the world. Mankind . . . [is now] split into believers and unbelievers, and this cleavage was to continue beyond the grave.[7]

Meanwhile, Europe was very restless for trade. Venice pursued commercial relations with Muslim Cairo, which had access to Asia through the Red Sea, while Genoa unsuccessfully attempted to establish contacts with Asia through another Muslim power, Iran, which controlled the Persian gulf. Many Genoans also had close relations with Portugal, which was engaged in mortal conflict with Iberian Muslims. In those days, Prince Henry the Navigator (d. 1460), a son of King John I of Portugal and a fanatic anti-Muslim, was training a sizable number of mariners, including some Genoans, for ocean voyage with the assumption that the only way to establish direct trade with Asia, evading the Muslim middlemen, was to find an ocean route around Africa. Pope Nicholas V gave him the right to claim all discoveries up to India in 1454. This permission was confirmed in the following year by Pope Calixtus III. Meanwhile, Christian forces managed to overpower Iberian Muslims between 1481 and 1492; they also drove out the Jews along with Muslims. It so happened that 1492 was the year when the Genoan, Christopher Columbus (d. 1506), sailed for North America with the support of Isabella I, the Catholic of Castile, and Ferdinand II, the Catholic of Aragon. In 1494, Portugal and Spain agreed that a line 370 leagues west of Cape Verde Island would serve as the demarcation of their respective zones. This agreement received the papal approval of Alexander VI as the line dividing the discoveries of Portugal and Spain. In accordance with this agreement, Vasco da Gama (d. 1525) of Portugal set sail from the Iberian shore in 1497, reaching the Indian Ocean by way of the

Point of Good Hope in 1498, much to the joy of Portugal. (With the defeat of Iberian Muslim forces, feudalism gave way to absolute monarchy in Spain, as exemplified by the rule of Ferdinand and Isabella.)

*   *   *   *   *

The Iberian peninsula held a significant place as a cultural and political hub and as the heartland of the Counter Reformation in the sixteenth century. The ethos and character of the Iberian kingdoms which initiated the ascendancy of the West may be illustrated by the colorful life of Charles V (even though he lived shortly after the beginning of the Western expansion). Charles V (1500-1558), emperor of the Holy Roman Empire, concurrently held the Spanish throne (as the grandson of Ferdinand and Isabella), and his reign covered France, Holland, Germany, Austria, the Kingdom of Naples, as well as overseas territories. It is said that he had four chief adversaries, i.e., Turkish Muslims, German Protestants, King Francis I of France, and the papacy; he made appropriate compromises by playing ball with the lesser evil as the occasion required.

To Emperor Charles, the Holy Roman Empire represented the Islam-inspired synthesis of religion (Western Catholicism of the Counter Reformation tradition), culture (Iberian-based European system), and socio-political order (absolute monarchy, designed to reign over Europe, and potentially the whole world). Understandably, he had no sympathy for Martin Luther and other Reformers who intended to "reform" the priority of the Western church. Accordingly, he summoned Luther before the Diet of Worms in 1521 and condemned him by his imperial edict. (Luther, however, was kept in safe seclusion by his protector and sympathizer, the Elector of Saxony.) Adrian VI (pope 1522-1523) also denounced Luther as a destructive element within Christendom. Charles then pressured Pope Adrian to expel the emperor's enemy, Francis I of France, from Italy, and made Francis swear allegiance to the throne by the Treaty of Madrid in 1526. Soon, however, Francis rebelled and waged war against Charles with the backing of Venetians and the new pope (Clement VII). Significantly, although emperor Charles was fanatically anti-Protestant and pro-Catholic, he had no qualms about taking the pope as a prisoner. Also, because of the war against France, Venice, and the papacy, Charles needed the support of German princes and electors, hence he decided not to press charges against Luther. Instead, it was agreed in 1529 that each German state could decide its own religious preference and affiliation—Roman Catholicism or Protestantism. But Charles blamed Luther for the "Protestant" rebellions (especially the uprising of the Rhenish knights) and condemned him again at the Diet of Augsburg in 1530. Unfortunately for Charles, the Turkish Muslim forces about that time threatened the city of Vienna, then a part of Charles' empire. France then allied with the Turks. Thus, again, Charles needed the support of Germany and did nothing against Luther. Charles declared war against the Turks in 1535 and against France the following year. This intermittent war with Franco-Turkish forces continued until 1544.

In 1545, Charles persuaded Pope Paul III to call the Council of Trent, a Council which the Protestants refused to attend. The Protestant action pleased Charles since it gave him an excuse to use military means against the Protestants. Thus Emperor Charles declared the Schmalkadic War, the first religious war in Germany, in 1546. Although Charles claimed military victory over the Protestants, this war signified the emperor's political downfall, and he was compelled to recognize the Protestants as stipulated by the Peace of Augsburg in 1555.

*   *   *   *   *

To the people in the Iberian kingdoms, colonialism was not simply a commercial, military, religious, or cultural undertaking, it was the combination of all these and much more. And, just as they did not question that it was God's will to eliminate Muslims in the Iberian peninsula, they were also under "divine mission" to conquer all non-Christian people. By that time, Europeans had transferred their anti-Muslim image to all other non-Christians. "In fact," says William Sweet, "the early *conquistadores* considered themselves Christian crusaders and brought over to the New World the ideas which had grown up in the long wars which they had fought against the Moors in Spain, using the same battle cries and evoking the same saints in the New World that had served them in the old."[8] In short, colonialism was an instrument for Christian expansion, and vice versa. In their eyes, presumably "Christian" ends justified all kinds of questionable means.

Both Portugal and Spain believed that their 1494 agreement to divide the whole world into two halves, as it were, gave each of them room to maneuver. Thus, Portugal—following the footsteps of Vasco da Gama—proceeded to establish an overseas empire, claiming India, the East Indies, Brazil, and later on, East Asia. Spain, following Columbus' route, proceeded to the West Indies, Cuba, Mexico, South America, and the Florida Coast. In 1565, Philip II of Spain (the so-called "most Catholic of kings") established a Spanish settlement in the Philippines via Mexico.

As might be expected, the ascendancy of two Roman Catholic powers, Spain and Portugal, provided a ready-made channel for the papacy to become involved in the work of Christian evangelism through the practice of patronage (*patronato* in Spanish; *padronado* in Portuguese)—concessions granted to monarchs by popes for the service of the church. As early as 1492, when Muslim forces in Granada were defeated, Pope Sixtus IV gave the Spanish crown the right of patronage over all reconquered, and in 1493 Pope Alexander VI commissioned Ferdinand and Isabella to send missionaries by means of patronage to the New World. Alexander's bull in 1501 specifically "allowed the monarchs to collect tithes in the colonies and to use the money to defray the cost of christianization." In 1508 Julius II "allowed the Spanish crown to name the candidates for all ecclesiastical offices . . . in the Indies. . . ."[9]

Rome tried to maintain a measure of ecclesiastical control over churches in overseas areas, sometimes sending its own missionaries (usually members of religious orders) to overseas churches, though

Portuguese officials in India, for example, usually ignored or imprisoned them. During the initial period of Western expansion, the patronage system was utilized more by civil officials to enhance the authority and prestige of the monarchs than the other way around, though some strong personalities among the religious orders managed to act quite independently of civil officials. From the beginning, Spanish missionaries in the Americas and in the Philippines, much as some of the Islamic communities had done previously with non-Muslims, incorporated the entire non-Christian people into the general framework of the Spanish cultural synthesis and then gradually converted them afterward. The Portuguese missionaries, on the other hand, tried to convert a smaller number of non-Christian individuals, reorienting them to believe and act like the Portuguese, and hoped that through the "ripple effect" the Portuguese-Christian influence might penetrate the larger non-Christian world. The deliberate but time-consuming approach of the Portuguese missionaries underwent a complete overhaul, however, with the coming of Francis Xavier (d. 1552) and his fellow Jesuits, whose attitudes were much closer to those of the Spanish friars.

Xavier, a nobleman from Navarre, a recognized leader of the Counter Reformation and a charter member of the Society of Jesus, arrived in India in 1541 as Apostolic Nuncio. Because of his Iberian experience, Xavier was anti-Islamic, and so was naturally uncomfortable in an India ruled partly by the Muslim Mughal dynasty (1526-1761). His stays at Molucca and Malacca (1544-1548) and in Japan (1549-1551) were much happier years for him. Throughout his days in Asia, Xavier urged Portuguese authorities to cooperate with the objective of evangelism. Part of his great success as an evangelist was due to his efforts to convert the leaders and elites in society through non-Christian, especially Buddhist, idioms and symbols. All in all, Xavier had an unusually successful missionary career in Japan.

In 1575, the newly arrived Jesuit visitor, Alessandro Valignano, began to promote more independence of missionaries from the Portuguese patronage system. It was Valignano who articulated the policy of "accommodation" both for Japan and China. In China, he concluded that the Portuguese priests, who were there before him, were too ethnocentric and conservative. He drafted new recruits from Italy, including the famous missionary-scientist, Matteo Ricci (d. 1610), to carry out his new policies. At that time, Japan was being united by Toyotomi Hideyoshi (d. 1598) who was threatening to invade China. The Ming dynasty was naturally very anxious, but the incompetent Wan-li Emperor (r. 1572-1620), not knowing what to do, did nothing. The episode was concluded only by Hideyoshi's death. Meanwhile, Ricci, who had excellent training and ability in philosophy, the humanities, and the sciences, sufficiently impressed many influential people to be made a stipendiary of the court toward the end of his life. Ricci, following Valignano, was persuaded that Christianity in China should incorporate some of the Confucian rites, much to the horror of conservative missionaries in China and myopic theologians and canon lawyers in Europe. The so-called "rites-controversy," centering around this issue, lasted until the eighteenth century when the Vatican ruled against the participation of Chinese converts in their native rites. During Ricci's life, the Spanish armada was defeated and four popes died in less than two years.

Another Italian Jesuit, Robert de Nobili (1577-1656), advocated and practiced the policy of "adaptation" in Madura, India. Abandoning European ways, he identified himself almost completely with the Brahmin ascetic. It is said that he baptized over 600 high-caste Hindus, but his policy was condemned by his fellow missionaries and superiors. In 1622, Rome established the Congregation for the Propagation of the Faith (*Congregatio de Propaganda Fide*) in order to coordinate and centralize missionary activities under the papacy, to avoid excessive dependence on the patronage of Spain and Portugal, and to counteract the "errors" of such policies as "accommodation" and "adaptation." The Congregation's use of French missionaries, however, caused new frictions between Iberian and French missionary personnel. The cardinals who were in charge of the Congregation were directly accountable to the pope. In theory, this Congregation handled all matters connected with the missions, regarded as those regions of the world where the hierarchy was not yet established, or where, if established, the church was still in its initial stage of development.[10] Later on, however, the Congregation was deprived of such sweeping authority over all missionary matters.

*   *   *   *   *

The Iberian kingdoms' domination of the non-Western world came to a symbolic end in 1588 with the defeat of Spain's invincible armada, the pride of Philip II (d. 1598). Philip was the only son of Emperor Charles V. He became a widower early and made a marriage of policy with Mary Tudor, Queen of England, who was at least ten years older than him. Much to his disgust, however, the English Parliament refused to crown him. After Mary's death in 1558, he failed to secure the hand of Elizabeth. He was well known as a fanatic Catholic partisan, and his inhuman rule coupled with excessive use of the Inquisition antagonized many, especially in the Netherlands, which became independent in 1579. The vacuum created by the downfall of Spain was quickly filled by the Dutch, who became a leading maritime and colonial power in the seventeenth century, competing with Iberian influence in South Africa, Asia, and the Americas. Also France, preoccupied though it was with internal affairs, began to take an active role in establishing itself in Canada, the West Indies, Guiana, parts of Africa, and India (and later on Southeast Asia). All in all, France did not become the leading colonial power, for it lacked consistent support of the government and suffered from the reluctance of French investors.

In the long run, England became the dominant colonial empire, succeeding the Iberian kingdoms. Except for the discovery of Newfoundland in 1497 and the founding of the Moscovy Company in 1553, England did not exhibit much interest in overseas expansion during the sixteenth century. With the granting of a charter to the East India Company in 1600, however, England became interested in overseas colonies, leading to the British expansion in the Americas, India, and Africa. British settlements were established in Virginia, Maryland, New England, Nova Scotia, and the West Indian islands. In the second half of the seventeenth century, the Hudson Bay Company was established to handle the lucrative trade for Britain. In India, the East India Company initially controlled some of the coastal cities, e.g., Madras and Bombay, but after the fall of the Mughal Muslim dynasty in 1707 it began to compete with France for the dominion of the entire Indian sub-continent. By the time of the Treaty of Paris in 1763, England expanded its power in India, and later controlled the Straits, e.g., Penang, Singapore, and Malacca. Serious British expansion into Africa followed. Although the British empire lost the thirteen North American colonies, British colonial expansion continued in Australia, New Zealand, Trinidad, and Ceylon. After the Napoleonic wars (1799-1815), England gained such strategic spots as Tobago, Malta, and St. Lucia. Other European nations were also involved in the colonial expansion. During the eighteenth century, even such a tiny nation as Denmark took an active part in the "Black slave trade," side by side with Britain, France, and the Netherlands. For the most part, fierce colonial rivalry subsided during the first half of the nineteenth century, or so it was widely believed.

Fresh colonial rivalries flared up during the period between 1875 and World War I between the established colonial nations, England, France, the Netherlands, Portugal and Spain, and the newcomers, e.g., Russia, Germany, Belgium, Italy, the United States, and Japan. This new type of colonial competition was exemplified by the penetration into China, which theoretically preserved its political independence.[11]

Thus, colonialism during the past 450 years brought about three kinds of results. (i) Europeans migrated into North America, Australia, New Zealand, etc., all of which became virtual extensions of Europe, culturally and religiously. (ii) In Central and South America, the West Indies, and the Philippines, the mixture of Europeans and natives produced "new" peoples and cultures. (iii) Parts of Asia, Africa, and the Middle East were subjugated politically and economically by European powers, but were not heavily settled by Europeans. Accordingly, their cultural and religious traditions were not replaced by those of the Europeans. We will now consider how this has been experienced by the people of Asia.

Western Civilization and the Protestant World Mission

Christian evangelism and the dissemination of Iberian-European civilization were one and the same thing. Just as both countries sought to monopolize all the wealth and power they could secure overseas, both also made an attempt to monopolize religion and culture. They were not, however, always successful. Thus when the Jesuit visitor Alessandro Valignano (d. 1606) decided to send a Japanese Mission, consisting of four converted noble youths, to Portugal and Italy in 1582, he wanted to make certain that these delegates were to be closely supervised during their visit to Europe. As Lach observes, "they were not to learn anything of Christian division and especially nothing about Protestantism. Their tour was to be carefully chaperoned and of limited duration so that they would receive only the best possible impression of Catholic Europe."[12]

Despite the Iberians' sincere effort to perpetuate the medieval synthesis, the rest of Europe had already left the Middle Ages behind. As Sansom points out:

> By 1600, when many missionaries to Japan had come and gone, the Renaissance was in full swing all over Europe. . . . Those were the days when Leonardo da Vinci had laid the foundation of the experimental method and therefore of modern scientific inquiry; Copernicus had taught a new theory of the Universe; Harvey had lighted on the circulation of the blood; and Gilbert had commenced the study of electricity. But since these discoveries were unpalatable to the Inquisition, . . . it is unlikely that the Japanese gained any inkling from the missionaries. . . .[13]

Yet as significant as the Renaissance was, it was only one phase of a long process of gradual change in the West. The early Christian apologists had attempted to equate empirical history with the "history of salvation," a concept they learned from Judaism. Following this line of thinking, Augustine (d. 430), who held that Christianity began at the birth of the human race, divided human history into three periods: before the fall, under the law, and under Christ.

Augustine's scheme was modified by the Cistercian abbot, Joachim of Fiore (d. 1202), into an overlapping system of three ages: the age of the Father, from Adam to John the Baptist; the age of the Son, from the eighth century B.C. Judean King Uzziah to the mid-thirteenth century; and the age of the Holy Spirit, from the time of St. Benedict to the golden age of the future. Unlike Augustine, who believed that the "end" would take place beyond human history, Joachim was persuaded that the future, which was to be the age of justice and freedom, would be actualized within the time span of empirical history. It was this view of history, as explicated by Joachim, that was appropriated by August Comte (d. 1857) in his three-fold scheme of the stages of history: the mythico-religious, the philosophical speculative, and the scientific.[14] The rationalist emphasis of the Renaissance was amplified further by Romanticism, especially by the alluring exposition of Jean Jacques Rousseau (d. 1778) whose ideology, according to Christopher Dawson, was accepted by many as the new "moral basis of Western Society and the spiritual aspiration of Western culture."[15] In short, the rationalism we associate with the Enlightenment period had predecessors in antiquity and immediate successors in the nineteenth century as well. It was not an isolated movement.

Needless to say, the Enlightenment would not have taken place but for the contributions of Humanism, the Renaissance, and the Protestant Reformation.

Humanism bred the experimental sciences, . . . the Renaissance rediscovered much of classic culture and in so doing revived the notion of *man as creative being*; the Reformation . . . challenged the monolithic authority of the church. . . . The successful application of reason to any question depended on its correct application. . . . Such a methodology was most spectacularly achieved in the sciences and mathematics, where the logics of induction and deduction made possible the creation of a sweeping new cosmology. . . . The

Enlightenment [also] produced the first modern secularized theories of psychology and ethics. . . .[16]

Clearly modern Westerners, through the Renaissance and the Enlightenment, were formulating a new modern European religious-cultural-social-political synthesis which can be referred to simply as modern European civilization.

In response to Western colonialism, the elites of some Asian nations, as John Girling astutely observes, "adopted certain practices of colonialism primarily in order to *escape* colonialism."[17] Girling describes the intensely "Westernized" and yet "independent" Thailand of the late nineteenth century as follows: "The Thai policy was thereby reorganized according to the pattern of colonial administration—the monarch taking the place of the colonial governor—while the economy, or an important part of it, was integrated into the international capitalist system. This worldwide system, though far from being internally harmonious, was of course dominated by the same colonial powers, including America, whose representatives (the foreign advisors) were working so thoroughly to 'modernize' Siam."[18]

The Protestant World Mission

Unlike Spanish and Portuguese monarchs of the sixteenth century who were devoted to Catholicism and were willing to be responsible for evangelistic activities under the patronage system, many monarchs of the so-called "Protestant" colonial nations in the seventeenth and eighteenth centuries were not only indifferent to evangelism but tended to be hostile to the cause of Christian world mission. In the main, the "Protestant" churches in those days, many of them state churches, were preoccupied with internal problems and regarded the spiritual welfare of colonial subjects as the responsibility of their governments.

There was, however, a small group of Protestants, the "Pietists," who rejected the modern Europeans' notion of themselves and the *de facto* religion of secularized salvation. They hoped to rejuvenate their churches by forming small circles of spiritual vitality, referred to as the *ecclesiola in ecclesia*, within the larger church body. The Pietism advocated by such people as Philip Jacob Spener of Halle (d. 1705) did not have many followers in Germany, although it did influence the Moravians. But Pietism had many supporters in Denmark and it allied with the British Evangelical movement, which stressed the authority of the Bible, salvation by faith, and the work of the Holy Spirit.

It was the combined influence of continental Pietism and English Evangelicals, not the monarchs or the church authorities, that promoted the cause of the Protestant world mission. In this situation, as Cnattingius points out: "Protestant missionary enthusiasm had to find some fresh form for the organization of its missionary activity. The form it found was the private missionary societies.... They were simply associations of individual Christians, both clergy and laymen, who had felt the great call to take up missionary service and banded themselves together to form missionary undertakings overseas."[19] This is more or less how missionary societies of the seventeenth century, e.g., the Society for the Propagation of the Gospel in Foreign Parts and its parent body, the Society for Promoting Christian Knowledge, emerged. The eighteenth century witnessed the rise of the Methodist movement, the establishment of the Church Missionary Society, and the London Missionary Society. Soon Protestants in other nations also took active interest in world mission. Thus, "by the end of the Nineteenth century, almost every Christian body, from the Orthodox Church of Russia to the Salvation Army, and almost every country, from the Lutheran Church of Finland, . . . to the newest sects in the United States, had its share in the missionary enterprise overseas."[20]

Despite the initial hostility of the colonial governments toward the missionary movement, they began to be convinced that Christianity was an integral ingredient of Western civilization, which they wanted to propagate among colonial people. The colonial regimes also began to count heavily on the educational and philanthropic activities of missionaries for the same reason. For their part, many missionaries preferred to accept the powerful and influential colonial regimes rather than buck against them, and some also came to be persuaded that since it was not possible to present the pure Gospel anyway, they could at least present Western civilization, enriched as it was by Christianity. Thus the holy or unholy alliance between colonialism and Christian world mission developed and produced one great synthesis of this-worldly Christianity, Western civilization (supported by Western science and technology), capitalistic social order (with a built-in paternalism), and colonial political order—the entire synthesis cosmically legitimated by the global spread of Christianity. Christian evangelism thus came to mean "Westernization of the non-Western world," in keeping with the motto made famous by David Livingstone of the double aims of commerce (colonialism) and Christianity. It was very tempting for Westerners to think that sooner or later the whole world would be "Westernized," and that in the meantime at least the Western mode of thinking, supported by Western sciences, industry, business, technology, and a global transportation and communication system, would provide the necessary universal mental framework for men and women of the future to prosper.

Even with the powerful support of colonialism and the strong tide of westernization, the Christian world mission encountered numerous difficulties in Asia. The unkind caricature of Western missionaries, with Bible in one hand and toothbrush in the other, hardly portrayed the complexity of missionary problems, especially in many parts of Asia where other, and older, religions and philosophies prevailed. Unfortunately, many missionaries, especially those of Protestant groups, were not trained to deal with the religious, cultural, and political traditions in Asia. As early as 1940, William Ernest Hocking contrasted the poor quality of Protestant missionaries with the intellectual maturity of Jesuit missionaries in India, who had taken the trouble to learn the deeper sources of the life around them—"poised, unhurried, with firm judgment and far vision . .," whereas "our Protestant institutions are set for prompt delivery of partly prepared men. . . . The real lack, among Protestants, is a lack of perception . . . [and] a supposition that *we already know enough,* and that *more thinking is a luxury that can be dispenced with.*"21 The statistics-conscious missionaries tried to gain numbers of converts by approaching the people of least resistance. They resorted to establishing "mission compounds" for native converts so as to keep them away from their old "pre-Christian" environment. Equally discouraging was the confusion of Christianity and Western civilization, the unrivalled authority of the missionaries, both in religious and non-religious affairs, and the common human frailty of Western missionaries that led them to hang on to the leadership of the younger churches instead of cultivating indigenous initiative.

As for the United States' participation, the first American ship, *Empress of China,* sailed to China in 1785. Initially, the United States was primarily interested in trade—"clippers carried cargoes of rum, beans, and hardware to the Pacific Coast, where they were traded for furs. The furs were exchanged in China for silk, tea, porcelain, and furniture which sold at a good profit in America."22 After the Treaty of Nanking (1842) between England and China, the U.S., France, and Russia secured similar treaties of entry to China, and in 1854 Commodore Matthew Perry concluded, by force, the treaty with Japan. In the latter half of the nineteenth century, the United States became one of the new colonial powers. After the war with Spain in 1898, Spain ceded to the U.S. Cuba, Puerto Rico, Guam, and the Philippine Islands. In 1900, Hawaii was taken over as a new U.S. Territory. The U.S. now became a full-fledged Asian power. In 1900, the U.S. advocated the Open Door policy in China; the U.S. also sent troops to participate in the international expedition to Peking in order to quash the Boxer Rebellion. After the Russo-Japanese War (1904-5), the U.S. was instrumental in arranging a peace treaty between Russia and the new Asian imperialist power, Japan. Throughout the early twentieth century, the U.S. exerted tremendous power in maintaining "privileges" in China, especially in Shanghai where the U.S. and England supported each other, effectively dominating the Shanghai International Settlement.

Not surprisingly, the U.S. became an important agent—and, to many, an idealistic wing—of the westernization movement in Asia. However, the lack of consistent U.S. attitude and policy toward Asia has often baffled Asians. After all, it was difficult for the Chinese to feel that the U.S. was one and the same nation when they learned that, on the one hand, that before 1863, 108,471 laborers had been "Shanghaied" and sent to San Francisco,[23] and, on the other hand, a treaty was signed between China and the U.S. in 1868, cordially recognizing "*the inherent and inalienable right of man to change his home and allegiance,* and also the mutual advantage of the free migration and emigration of their citizens and subjects respectively from the one country to the other. . . ."[24] In any case, there is no question that the U.S. took a very active role in the westernization of Asia, especially by propagating the "American way of life" in commerce, education, and technology.

From the Asian perspective, the U.S. exhibited similar contradictory attitudes towards the Christian world mission. In the latter half of the nineteenth century, Edwin Arnold's *Light of Asia* (published in England in 1879), containing his rhapsodic biography of the Buddha, boasted 80 editions in America. In 1886, Henry Adams and John La Farge travelled to Japan "in search of Nirvana."[25] In 1893, the World's Parliament of Religions in Chicago invited representatives of non-Western religions for the first time into Western society. Yet the Student Volunteer Movement for Foreign Missions attracted many at the turn of the century for the evangelization of the whole world. Moreover, starting with the Baptists (in 1814), many denominational groups organized missionary societies. And from 1910 onward, American Christians began to take leadership roles in various global missionary conferences.

The early twentieth century witnessed an era of transition from the frontier to the factory, as characterized by Frederick J. Turner. American Christianity developed two diametrically opposed wings—conservative Fundamentalism and liberal Social Gospel. Inevitably, the American missionary enterprise overseas, too, reflected theological divisions at home. In 1930, a group of Christian laymen established a commission to appraise the effectiveness of overseas missions called "A Laymen's Enquiry after One Hundred Years." The commission's report, *Re-thinking Missions*, was published in 1932.[26] This report was bitterly attacked by Hendrik Kraemer of Leiden at the missionary conference in Madras.[27] But before further debate had a chance to take place, World War II broke out.

Notes

1   See A.H. Johns, "Islam in Southeast Asia," Eliade, *The Encyclopedia of Religion*, VII, 406.

2   Nigel Cameron, *Barbarians and Mandarins* (New York: Walker/Weatherhill, 1970), 28-60.

3   R. Grousset, *The Rise and Splendour of Chinese Empire* (Berkeley: University of California Press, 1952), 246.

4   On this fascinating subject, consult Helene Wieruszowski, *The Medieval University* (Princeton: D. Van Norstrand, 1966).

5   Haas, *Destiny of the Mind*, 18, FN 1.

6   Vera M. Dean, *The Nature of the Non-Western World* (New York: The New American Library, 1957), 15.

7   G.E. von Grunebaum, ed., *Unity and Variety in Muslim Civilization* (Chicago: University of Chicago Press, 1955), 21.

8   W.W. Sweet, "Christianity in the Americas," in A.G. Baker, ed., *A Short History of Christianity* (Chicago: University of Chicago Press, 1940), 227.

9   A.J. Nevin, "Patronato Real," in S. Neil et al., eds., *Concise Dictionary of the Christian Mission* (Nashville: Abingdon Press, 1971), 474.

10 R. Hoffman, "Propaganda, Sacred Congregation of," in *ibid.*, 499.

11 On various powers' penetration of China, see "European Overseas Exploration and Empires," *The New Encyclopaedia Britannica, Macropaedia*, 15th edition, 1985, XVIII, 883A.

12 Donald F. Lach, *Asia in the Making of Europe*, (Chicago: The University of Chicago Press, 1965), II, 691.

13 G.B. Sansom, *Japan: A Short Cultural History* (New York: D. Appleton-Century, 1943), 453.

14 See N.E. Fehl, *History and Society* (Hong Kong: Chung Chi College, 1964), 14-15.

15 C. Dawson, *Enquiries into Religion and Culture* (London: Sheed and Ward, 1933), 150.

16 "Enlightenment," *The New Encyclopaedia Brittanica, Micropaedia*, 15th edition, 1985, IV, 504; my italics.

17 Girling, *Thailand*, 47-48.

18 *Ibid.*, 46.

19 II. Cnattingius, *Bishops and Societies* (London: S.P.C.K., 1952), 4.

20 S. Neill, *The Christian Society* (New York: Harper and Row, 1952), 203.

21 W.E. Hocking, *Living Religions and A World Faith* (New York: Macmillan, 1940), 207; my italics.

22 C.A. Bain, *The Far East* (Ames: Littlefield, Adams, and Company, 1952), 39.

23 Panikkar, *Asia and Western Dominance*, 141.

24 Konvitz, *The Alien and the Asiatic*, 5; the author's italics.

25 A.E. Christy, ed., *The Asian Legacy and American Life* (New York: John Day, 1942), 44.

26 The Commission of Appraisal, *Re-thinking Missions* (New York: Harper and Brothers, 1932).

27 See Hendrik Kraemer, *The Christian Message in a Non-Christian World* (London: The Edinburgh House, 1938).

Chapter Four

Spiritual Liberation and Freedom
in Asia

Asia under Western Domination

It may be worth reiterating my intention to portray in this volume three layers of the mental universe of Asians—the first referring to the ancient Asians' cosmological "world of meaning"; the second referring to Asians' mixed memory of Western domination, which in many ways destroyed the ancient Asian legacies and attempted to reshape Eastern cultures and societies according to Western paradigms. It is my intention now to discuss the third stratum of this mental universe; such a discussion is indeed a hazardous undertaking.

Many observers of contemporary Asia, especially those in the West, tend to advance such simplistic formulas as the "struggle for Westernization of the East" or the "conflict between modernization and the residues of ancient tradition." Undoubtedly, these formulaic views may describe some aspects of contemporary Asia. But it is quite misleading to dismiss inherited Eastern cultures and religions merely as those which have been "identified with a stagnating society," and which therefore act "as a tremendous force for social inertia."[1] The contemporary Asian situation has been shaped by at least three factors: (i) the destructive impact of the West, which repudiated the fabric of Eastern culture in favor of those of the Western model, followed by the Asians' painful struggle for political (and to some extent) cultural independence; (ii) the post-war (World War II) Asians' experience of renewed confidence in themselves and in things Eastern, including the new phenomenon of Eastern influence on the West, tempered though by resignation about the persistence of the Western impact on Asia; and (iii) a futuristic outlook, with the conviction of the necessity of holding in balance the traditional Eastern ideal of spiritual liberation and the new aspiration for human freedom, together with the as-yet very dim awareness that such an ideal will be possible only when other non-Asians, including of course Westerners, are also able to achieve their own spiritual-human synthesis. Although by necessity these three factors must be dealt with as though they were separable phenomena, in reality they are closely related. Let us first briefly reexamine the first fact, namely, the destructive phase of the impact of the West, and the Asians' response, i.e., their struggle for independence from the Western yoke.

* * * * *

Earlier it was pointed out that the ancient ideal of Asia was the integration of all values as well as the balance and harmony of diverse groups within society into a seamless whole. In such a setting, society had a certain fluidity, maintained not by law or force but by mores and customs which were shared. Evidently, part of the reason for the erosion of Asian society around the time of the West's ascendancy was due to the Tokugawa feudal regime (1603-1867) and the Manchu Ch'ing dynasty (1644-1912) imposing alien political and legal principles while intending to uphold traditional culture. The cultural fragmentation of Asian people, caused by the government-imposed political and legal rigidity, offered an easy prey to the advancing West.

The influence of the West did not penetrate directly at first to the level of the masses, but it fostered the development of three kinds of "elites," who competed for the souls of the masses. (a) Traditional elites, who were determined to preserve, and to restore if need be, ancient Asian mores, values, cultures and religions, and understandably resented anything novel or western. (b) New elites with westernized education, mostly young and urban, determined to replace the "dead weight," as many of them characterized traditional Eastern culture, with new Western models. They were not vanguards of colonial governments, as they were often accused by traditional elites, but they were converts to Western civilization, i.e., the pseudo religion of secularized salvation with science, democracy, technology, and "progress" in the supra-national capitalistic economic network. Not surprisingly, some of them embraced the Christian faith, and later sizable Christian communities developed in Asia. It must be pointed out that in their own minds, these new elites were committed patriots. They merely examined traditional Eastern society through the eyes of Western civilization and hoped to reshape and redirect their own "stagnant" society with the infusion of Western values, ideologies and institutions. (c) In between the traditional and new elites was a small group of another kind whom I once called, for the lack of a better nomenclature, "modern Asian religious reformers."[2] Most of them had Westernized educations but, unlike new elites, they had the unshakable conviction that traditional Eastern values, mores, religions, and cultures had enough hidden vitality to serve as adequate resources for Asians in the modern world. They were suspected by the traditional elites, who thought they were too modern or Westernized, while they were condemned by the new elites for being too traditional. All three types of Asian elites aspired to influence the masses with their own scenarios for the future of Asia, but in the early twentieth century it appeared that the tide of Westernization was going to continue for many more years to come.

The global situation as well as the destiny of Asian people changed a great deal with World War I (1914-1918). Until then, as Hans Morgenthau rightly observed, there existed "in the Western world a community of moral principles and moral conduct, a community of fundamental religious beliefs, a common way of life—in one word, a common civilization."[3] But a Serbian's assassination of the Austrian Archduke in 1914 ushered in a chain reaction of threats and counter-threats that eventually involved all the major powers in Europe (England, France, Russia, Italy) and Britain's

East Asian ally, Japan (and later the United States) as allies against
Austria-Hungary, Germany, and Turkey in World War I. When
the war broke out, many Asians—Hindus, Muslims, Buddhists,
etc.—fought with the Allies, not because they felt obligated to fight
for their colonial masters (as some Western defenders of colonialism insinuated), but for two great and contradictory reasons; first,
they had pious hopes that the Western Allies were right in fighting
this war "to end all wars," and second, by fighting on the side of the
Allies, their own lot would greatly improve in the post-war period.
(Understandably, it was especially hard for Asian Muslims to fight
against their fellow Muslims in Turkey.) For the most part, the
Asians learned four great lessons in World War I. (i) Obviously,
the war signified the erosion of the European moral community.
(ii) The introduction of many new deadly weapons, e.g., Zeppelin
airships, tanks, poison gas, submarines, etc., was a horrendous
"means" if the Westerners really wanted to end warfare. Clearly
many people did not believe that it was possible to end warfare; "to
fight this war to end all wars" was just rhetoric. (iii) Notwithstanding their colonial masters' criticism, the Bolshevik Revolution in
Russia in 1917 might point to the eventual growth of the proletarian sense of community, which—more so than capitalistic-colonial
nations—could be empathic, and basically congenial, to the Asian
masses. (iv) Even though Woodrow Wilson's proposal for the
League of Nations was rebuffed by his own nation and not strongly
supported by his European friends, there was no question that the
U.S. surpassed European nations as a leading world power.

*   *   *   *   *

Impressed by these lessons, Sun Yat-sen (1866-1925), spiritual
father of the Chinese Republic, tried to forge a new form of nation
in China, based on "Three Peoples' Principles," without depending
on European powers but attempting to reconcile the political
democracy *à la* the U.S. and Russian economic democracy. To
him, the masses were not ignorant people to be guided but com-

rades-in-arms for the peace of the world, as the Chinese national anthem says:

San Min Chu I (Three People's Principles)

Our aim shall be
To found a free land
World Peace be our stand.

Lead on, comrades;
Vanguards ye are!
Hold fast your aim
By sun and by star!
Be earnest and brave
Your country to save.
One heart, one soul;
One mind, one goal.[4]

For other Asian nations, too, World War I marked the beginning of the erosion of Western colonialism—starting with the Islamic nations. A memorandum was presented to the Peace Conference by the Muslims in Asia after World War I, asking that they "be recognized as independent sovereign peoples under the guarantee of the League of Nations."[5] But the peace settlement was a great disappointment to the Asian Muslims. Moreover, "western political and economic controls in the Near and Middle East, and the disregard of Western political leaders for human and social interests, forced the nationalist leaders to devote all their energies to the struggle against Western domination."[6] And, as might be expected, much of the Near Eastern Muslims' sentiment was shared by Asian Muslims as well.

The period between the Two World Wars was an extremely complicated time for Asia. In hindsight, we can say that it was definitely a period of "Europe in Retreat," to borrow the phrase of K.M. Panikkar.[7] The most influential ideology of the time in Asia was the Wilsonian idealistic principle of the "self-determination of people," which enabled the old and new elites as well as the modern religious reformers to work together for the first time for the great cause of political justice. In India and other colonized areas in Asia, the new elites, long regarded by colonial officials as allies, began demanding political independence. After a British general ordered the army to fire on helpless civilians in Amritsar in 1919, Mahatma Gandhi, who had been trained in London and lived for some years in South Africa, became the head of a nationalist movement in India and began organizing the non-violent civil disobedience movement.[8] It was rumored that in 1942 Sir Stafford Cripps, in order to solicit India's support for the British war effort, promised to campaign for India's dominion status after the war. Twenty years earlier, such an offer would have meant something. But in 1942 Gandhi and others dismissed Cripps' offer as though it were a post-dated check on a bankrupt empire. Another Western-educated new elite, Jewaharlal Nehru, a scion of a Kashmir Brahman family, the bluest of the blue blood in India, sounded more like a modern religious reformer when he stated: "We are citizens of no mean country and we are proud of the land of our birth, of our people, our culture and traditions."[9]

It is more difficult to generalize about the so-called Buddhist nations in Asia. Of the Mahāyāna Buddhist nations, China will be discussed later. As to Japan, Vera Dean's shorthand description of it as "Asian Westernism" may be very appropriate.[10] Although Japan was still governed by the Tokugawa feudal regime in 1854, when Commodore Matthew Perry of the United States forced a Treaty for trade on it, the new architects of the Meiji imperial regime, which assumed the reign of the nation in 1868, were determined to import Western technology in order to become a rich and strong modern nation-state. In time Japan "inhaled" Western-type imperialism and aspired to become the leading nation in Asia. Sansom quotes a popular *Song of Diplomacy*, revealing how the Japanese felt:

> In the West there is England,
> In the North, Russia.
> My countrymen, be careful!

Outwardly they make treaties,
But you cannot tell
What is at the bottom of their hearts.
There is a Law of Nations, it is true,
But when the moment comes, remember,
The strong eat up the weak.[11]

As a brand-new imperialist power in Asia, Japan successfully pursued its goal, winning the Sino-Japanese War (1894-95) and Russo-Japanese War (1904-05); it annexed Korea in 1910 and profited from the alliance with England during World War I. After World War I Japan acquired some former German possessions in Asia in accordance with the League of Nations' mandate. In 1931, Japan started the Manchurian War, then invaded Central China the following year. In 1940, Japan joined Fascist Italy and Nazi Germany as one of the Axis powers, and entered World War II in 1941.

The picture is vastly different in the Theravāda Buddhist nations in South and Southeast Asia. Five (out of six) Theravāda Buddhist countries were directly subjugated to Western colonial regimes. In the main, the French officials (in charge of Cambodia and Laos, for example) allowed traditional Buddhist and village political organizations but discouraged their modernization, while the British officials (in, say, Burma) eliminated monarchy and discredited the indigenous aristocracy, while not opposing modernization.[12] Also in Burma, after the failure of the traditional-oriented Saya Sen rebellion in 1931, the independence movement began to take on new dimensions. A number of Western-educated, leftist intellectuals became involved and soon assumed the major responsibilities of leadership. These men recognized the need for an ideological framework which would be meaningful in the Burmese context, and gradually developed the concept of Buddhist socialism. . . ."[13]

When we discuss the independent movement of the Buddhist and non-Buddhist countries in Southeast Asia, we are reminded of the fact that, as Vera Dean succinctly states:

In the span of a few short months the era of Western colonialism was suddenly ended by the Japanese conquest of Southeast Asia in the early stages of the Pacific War. In spite of the brevity of Japanese military occupation . . . Southeast Asia emerged from it changed in so many vital respects that a return of Western colonialism after Japan's defeat was rendered very hazardous, if not impossible. . . .[The] visible destruction of Western prestige by a non-Western, Asian nation eradicated the age-old myth of Western supremacy. . . .[14]

* * * * *

For the most part, Asian people between the two world wars, convinced of the decline of the unified European moral community after World War I, kept watchful eyes on what might transpire in the West in the post-war period. The American proposal for the self-determination of the people and the Russian principle derived from the Bolshevik revolution were important to them as much needed critiques of modern European civilization. They felt that some features of both would be useful to Asia. Of course, the situation in various Asian nations was very different. For example, Japan clearly preferred the Western option to the Russian alternative; it began, however, to lean toward the Italian-German wing within Westernism in the 1930s. In Afghanistan, and to a great extent in Thailand, traditional religious, cultural, social, and political structures were so strong that they were not hospitable to new inspirations from abroad. In other Asian nations where people were fighting for independence, both the principle of self-determination and the goals of the Russian Revolution became important slogans for liberation. Many of them, e.g., the Indian soldiers who fought with the British in Europe during World War I, Indo-Chinese Labor Corps working during the immediate post-war period in the south of France, and Chou En-lai (d. 1976) and many other Asian students in Paris early in the 1920's, experienced serious disillusionment with modern European civilization. Also, they reacted quite differently to the Russian Revolution. As Panikkar points out: "in countries where the nationalist movements had already been in existence for a considerable time, like India, the communist theory gained but little support; but in Indonesia and Indo-China, where the movements for independence became effective in the period after the Russian Revolution, the Communists became a major factor in the forces working for liberation."[15] In various parts of Asia the movement for political independence, which had been greatly inspired by the principle of self-determination of the people, now acquired an economic dimension. The example of the Russian Revolution, which had transformed a backward economy into an advanced industrial civilization in a relatively short time, inspired many Asians. The Russian form of Communism, which found followers among small numbers of intellectuals, did not, however, capture the imagination of the masses. Thus the conservative Chiang Kai-shek (d. 1975) in the late 1920's took over the leadership of the hitherto pro-Communist Kuomintang party in China. (As is well known, the Chinese form of Communism led by Mao Tse-tung was more successful later on.)

Meanwhile, Asians' attitude toward the U.S., admiration coupled with envy, hatred, etc. was exacerbated by the inconsistency of the U.S. How could one reconcile the principle of the self-determination of the people, promoted by many Americans, with the 1917 barred zone provision, prohibiting immigration from India, Siam, Arabia, Indo-China, the Malay Peninsula, Afghanistan, New Guinea, Borneo, Java, Ceylon, Sumatra, Celebes, and various other parts of Asia?[16] It was difficult to reconcile the genuine humanitarian aid to Japan in 1923 following the Great Earthquake with the 1924 Quota Act, which was in fact the Japanese Exclusion Act.[17] Moreover, although most Asians subscribed to democratic principles, they could not fathom the coexistence of the very wealthy and the very poor within the same democratic society, and they were horrified by the misery of the Great Depression in the heartland of democracy.

I am sure that many Asians expected the bankruptcy of the European community to be followed by something new but were surprised by the emergence of Italian Fascism and German Nazism in European soil. In spite of these totalitarian regimes' claims to be on the side of the "have-nots," their visions did not inspire many people in Asia. Many Asians were surprised when Japan joined the ranks of Italy and Germany and were more dumbfounded to have Japanese militarists as their new colonial masters, during the early part of World War II. If nothing else, World War II demonstrated most dramatically that the phenomenon of Western colonialism in Asia, which had lasted 450 years from the time of Vasco da Gama, had ended.

Revolution and Tradition

The Asians' ambivalent post-war experience reveals their renewed confidence in themselves and in things Eastern, including their legitimate pride about the new phenomenon of the increasing Eastern influence in the West, but betrays the peculiar combination of impatience, resignation, and acknowledgement about the persistence of the Western influences on some aspects of Eastern life.

When I think of post-World War II in Asia, I often think of the title of Irving Kristol's perceptive article, "The Twentieth Century Began in 1945."[18] I share his observation that the nineteenth century, in which the "world of meaning" of the West dominated the main stage of world history, lasted longer than simply the year 1899. To the majority of the human race, which lives outside the Western world, it was not the year 1900 but the year 1945 that marked the significant line between two worlds of experience. Thus, most Asians (And I suspect Africans, too) feel, to again repeat Kristol's way of putting it, that *the twentieth century began only in 1945. In a real sense*, the emergence of independent Asian nations—the Philippines (1946), India and Pakistan (1947), Ceylon (Sri Lanka), Burma, South and North Korea (1948), Indonesia and the Peoples Republic of China (1949), South and North Vietnam (1954), Cambodia (1955), Laos (1956), Federation of Malaya (1957), Malaysia (1963), Bangladesh (1971), and the Socialist Republic of Vietnam (1975), etc.—not only signified the end of Western colonialism, but also represented what both caused and resulted from their political independence, namely, contemporary Asians' momentous redefinition of their senses of dignity, value, and freedom. But the Asian process of redefinition does not imply the universalization of Western concepts, as it is often misinterpreted in some Western circles. Considerations of human dignity, value, and freedom are today no longer only discussions within the European-inspired civilization and its spheres of influence. By tilting the balance politically, socioeconomically, socially, culturally and religiously, Asia is now making a serious attempt to retrieve important resources from its traditional "world of meaning." It does not imply, either, that contemporary Asians are rejecting Western influence altogether in attempting to return to the past of the East. Easterners (i.e., more in Japan, Korea, Taiwan, Singapore, the Philippines and less elsewhere) are appropriating certain features of Western civilization in order to enrich their own world of meanings. As we see the bewildering phenomenon of re-definition going on from Afghanistan in the West to Japan in the East, we realize that the ingredients as well as the ratio of the indigenous and Western elements are different, but the principles of the redefinition common to all are how to balance "revolutionary" and "traditionalizing" impulses in order to find coherent meaning in this chaotic epoch of world history.

We may recall the eloquent words of Pandit Nehru, made on the eve of India's independence: "Long ago we made a tryst with destiny, and now the time comes when we shall redeem our pledges, not wholly or in full sense, but very substantially. At the stroke of the midnight hour, when the world sleeps, India will awake to life and freedom. . . . It is fitting that at this solemn moment we take the pledge of dedication to the service of India and her people to a still larger cause of humanity."[19] In so stating, Nehru spoke for millions in Asia who had dedicated their life and energy to the cause of Asia's independence from Western colonialism. Little did they expect that with the attainment of political independence, they would face more serious and complex problems. In a way, the problem would have been much simpler for Asians if they could turn the clock backwards, as it were. Then they could simply erase the recent memory of humiliation and revert back to the ancient way of life. But that is impossible. Like the ancient Israelites who learned to live in Egypt or in Babylon, so the contemporary Asians consciously or unconsciously "inhaled" some of the ethos of an alien civilization—in their own lands—during the past two centuries of the colonial period. And, much as the ancient Israelites who tasted the splendor of great civilizations could no longer remain simple shepherds and farmers of Palestine, Asians have become accustomed to some aspects of Western life and thought.

Many Asians are now nostalgic for this period of struggle for independence, because then people of different religions and political persuasions felt united in a common goal. In a sense, the achievement of independence meant fulfillment, which sadly implied the end of the dream. Moreover, Asians were compelled to face the difficult relationships among nations within Asia. It became evident to many Asians that their national independence came at a time when the era of the nation-state was gradually taken over by the era of regional blocs. Thus, although no one was willing to give up national sovereignty, all felt the need for some sort of regional cooperation and collective security. Accordingly, Asian nations and new African nations wanted to develop some kind of unity, partly to counterbalance the pressures of Western and Communist blocs. With this in mind, twenty-nine Asian and African nations (with no "white" nations, including the U.S.S.R.), representing about 56 percent of the global population met in Bandung, Indonesia in 1955.[20] Sadly, in spite of the spirited talks of the conference, the so-called Bandung Front turned out to be a feeble alliance with very little to guide and inspire the life of its member nations.

In hindsight, it becomes clearer to us why the Bandung Front nations lacked feelings of unity. The historical insularity of various Asian cultures and societies—due largely to the historical affirmation of the pattern of juxtaposition—was probably an important reason. In the main, people underestimated the reality of the residual ties, even though in many cases such ties were not very visible; in consequence, the bonds between some of the new nations and the former colonial governments were not as easily cut off as the leaders of the new nations had hoped. For the former colonial powers, especially for those who thought colonialism would last forever, the end of their relationships with the new nations was too drastic. For example, some Dutch felt that their colonial policy in Indonesia "had been so progressive and enlightened that it assured the continued loyalty and contentment of the masses" of the Indonesian people.[21] Moreover, religious divisions reinforced political divisions, so that the practical cooperation between, for instance, Catholic Philippines (which incidentally had a sizable Muslim minority) and Muslim Indonesia, or between India (which too has a large Muslim population) and Muslim Pakistan proved to be difficult. Even within the so-called Buddhist nations of Southeast Asia, ancient hostilities still separated Thailand and Cambodia or Cambodia and Vietnam. Above all, each nation was protective of itself and was not open to the development of friendship with its neighbors. This was true even in the communist nations which came into existence in the post-war era, i.e., Mainland China, North Korea, and North Vietnam. In short, the same combination of revolutionary and traditional thrusts, which so successfully aligned many Asians for a common cause during the struggle for independence, tended to pull Asian societies in different directions after the war.

*   *   *   *   *

As early as 1961, Arnold Toynbee talked about a "double crisis" for the West—"an internal change in the structure of the Western world and a bigger and more important change in its relations to the huge, non-Western majority of the human race. The West had lost its previous supremacy in the world; and inside the West, Western Europe has lost its previous supremacy in the West as a whole."[22] Communism, the new power based in Eastern Europe, had earlier been characterized by Toynbee as Western heresy: "It was," in his opinion, "a Western criticism of the West's failure to live up to her own Christian principles in the economic and social life of this professedly Christian society."[23] World War I had both caused and signified the bankruptcy of the myth of the European moral community. Now World War II effectively destroyed the European state system—based on states of approximately equal strength—which had existed since the sixteenth century. Thus, fragmented Europe came to be threatened by the strength of the new super-state, the U.S.S.R. Meanwhile, the attempt to eliminate Fascism, Nazism, and Japanese militarism meant facing the menace of Communism's "Iron Curtain," so dramatically portrayed by Winston Churchill.

Out of the ruins of World War I, two figures, Wilson and Lenin, began to assume world leadership. Now, two decades later, Democracy and Communism, advocated by the U.S.A. and the U.S.S.R. respectively, confronted one another. Coming from the same modern Western tradition, they had many things in common, e.g., their concept of history, their intense this-worldly orientation, and their belief in progress. But they also represented "two hostile and incompatible systems of morality, politics, and society, both claiming a monopoly of virtue, universal validity, and universal dominion, the one being bound to destroy the other."[24] Many believe that the battleground of Democracy and Communism is in Europe, especially in economic, diplomatic and military spheres, as the U.S. policymakers have maintained. There are, however, MacMahon Ball and many others who are just as persuaded that the conflict between Democracy and Communism will be determined by the choice of the "uncommitted" nations of the Third World. "The choice these people make, whether it be to try to remain neutral, or whether it be to ally themselves with one side or the other, may tip the balance of world power."[25]

Some Westerners fail to understand that what is happening in Asia today is, as Harold Isaacs pointed out, "part of a gigantic rearrangement of continents and nations and classes in which we, too, a hemisphere away, are profoundly involved.[26] Likewise, many Asians cannot easily see world-wide issues like the post-war Communist expansion in eastern and central Europe and in other places. "Their outlook [is] overshadowed by past conflict with imperial power; for them the greater fear [is] the entrenching of colonialism, and not the advent of a new and aggressive expansion [of Communism]."[27]   Although many Westerners suspect that the ghost of Communism is under the bed of every social revolution that is shaking Asian society, Communism is qualitatively different from social revolution, nor did Communism bring it about. "What the Communists claim to do is to explain the revolution and to have the right of leading it to a successful end."[28]

Westerners have failed to acknowledge the simple distinction made by Hans Morgenthau and others that "in Europe we face Russian imperialism, but in Asia we face genuine revolution." Morgenthau further points out that the failure of Western nations to distinguish Communism from the Asian revolution resulted in the ineffectiveness of the specific measures taken by the Western democratic nations. "We have acted in Asia as though the threat that confronts us there were identical with the one we must meet in Europe."[29]   The main reason for such a failure on the part of the Westerners is not hard to find. As early as 1948, Toynbee had already pointed out that the West's inability to appreciate the meaning of the events in Asia as a part of the global revolution was due to the fact that "the West today is still looking at history from [her] old parochial self-centered standpoint." It was his impression that "all the world has now profited by an education which the West has provided, except . . . the West itself."[30]

One serious problem which the new Asian situation causes for the West is the poor readjustment of the former colonial nations. Although they had to swallow the reality of the political independence of Asian nations, they would still like to somehow continue their dominant influence in Asia. Moreover, as Fitzgerald rightly pointed out, democratic nations, particularly the U.S., obsessed with the dramatic clash of Communism and Democracy, are impatient of the theory of non-alignment, which is believed to be unrealistic and thus an element of weakness in the struggle against Communism."[31]   Many Westerners are unaware that Asians see three components in Western colonial imperialism—"political, economic, and cultural—which, incidentally, were the three main committees appointed by the Afro-Asian Conference held in Bandung in 1955.[32]   And, as far as Asian (and probably African, too) nations are concerned, now that political independence has been achieved, they must strive for "economic" and "cultural" independence. As Northrop astutely observed, the "cultural" component in Asia's fear of Western colonial imperialism is the one least understood in the West. He cited MacArthur's suggestion of Christianization of Japan with a battleship full of Western missionaries, and the effort to "convert the rest of the world to the American way of life" through a "hard-hitting Voice of America." "All such suggestions strike the Asian as demonstrating that America and the West are withholding a political imperialism and slightly restraining an economic one merely to impose an even more dangerous cultural one."[33]

Panikkar points out three issues of concern to those at the Bandung Conference. They were (i) "Colonialism and Communism," (ii) the principle of racial equality, and (iii) the issues pertaining to A- and H-bombs. Obviously, the principle of racial equality is a supremely important issue for African nations, but the conference wanted to proclaim to the whole world that "the doctrine of *apartheid* in South Africa is directed as much against Asians as against Africans. It will [also] be remembered . . . [that] in the U.N., India and other Asian countries have been fighting strenuously for the acceptance of the principle."[34] Doubtless, the principle of racial equality will remain one of the most crucial issues for the future of Western and Asian relations. Parenthetically, when the diaries of William Lyon Mackenzie King, the Prime Minister of Canada for over twenty years (1921-30, 1935-48), were published in 1976, it was largely unnoticed in the West. But many Asian papers quoted his comment on the atomic bombing of Hiroshima in 1945: "It is fortunate," he wrote, "that the use of the bomb should have been upon the Japanese rather than the white races of Europe."[35] It is impossible to estimate the harm this kind of statement causes for understanding between the West and Asia. Further misunderstanding arose when the two authoritarian regimes not invited to the Bandung Conference (i.e., the governments of Chiang Kai-shek in Taiwan and of Syngman Rhee of Korea) were supported financially and militarily by Western nations. Though such a policy was not meant to be an affront to other Asian nations, it caused many to wonder at the West's understanding of the Asian situation, all of which supports the unhappy observation, made shortly after World War II by Filipino Carlos Romulo, that "the Western powers *lost by default* the splendid opportunity of building upon such movements a program of increasing autonomy for the native inhabitants leading to the ultimate goal of [political, economic, and cultural] independence."[36]

I am impressed by Rostow's perceptive opinion that the American outlook in Asia has been colored by what he calls "the China neurosis." Although the Philippine islands came under American political control after America's war against Spain, that did not alter its traditional China-centered policy toward Asia. Many Americans, including businessmen, missionaries, and educators, have lived and worked in China during the past hundred years.[37] According to Rostow, since the early 1930's, "the considerable commercial, religious, educational, and security interests of the United States and China have met defeat."[38] The U.S. experienced its greatest setback in Asia with the fall of the Kuomintang regime and the emergence of the Communist government under Mao Tsetung. Subsequent events in Asia, such as the Korean and Vietnam wars, have not been encouraging from an American perspective. The sequence of events has made it difficult for the U.S. to divorce the post-war Asian situation from the menacing expansion of Communism.

* * * * *

Yet it is not that Communism is faring much better in Asia in the latter half of the twentieth century, as some Western observers have hastily concluded. Seen from the West (either from the perspective of Democracy or that of Communism), "the great contest in Asia is between the totalitarian and democratic approach to the development of backward areas," as observed by Adlai Stevenson.[39] Both the leaders of Democracy and of Communism assume that the "Westernization of the East" during the past two centuries was so thorough that Asians now think and act like modern Westerners without considering their traditional "world of meaning." And both the Communist and Democratic nations attempt to woo Asians politically (offering various treaties) and economically (in terms of economic and military aid). From the Asian perspective, the issue is not so much which side (Communism or Democracy) offers better political and economic deals, but how Asians can—on their own—reorient not only the political structure (as they have done mostly since World War II) but the economic (e.g., land reforms, for example), demographic (population control), industrial and "cultural" fabrics of Asia as well. In other words, what Asia is seeking is a new religious-cultural-social-political synthesis based on some "new coherence." In this situation, Isaacs points out that Communism offers "a coherence of a kind" (based on Marxist ideology) whereas the Western Democratic world "has not yet been able to define what new coherence *it* might find to succeed its age of [colonialism]."[40]

The initial advantage of Communism was that it presented itself as an ally of nationalism and anti-colonialism. Such articles as "British Rule in India" by Marx and "On Colonialism" by Marx and Engels were read widely in Asia during the period of struggle for political independence.[41] Nevertheless, Communism's political record in Asia has been very mixed. In the late 1920's, conservative Chiang Kai-shek overcame Communist elements in the Kuomintang party in China. Ironically, it was Mao Tse-tung, whom Moscow had once rebuffed for not being an orthodox Communist, who consolidated Mainland China in 1949, and as Morgenthau notes: "its rise to power within China owes little to the Soviet Union, nor will it need to rely upon Russian support to maintain itself in power."[42] Thus, politically China will compete with the U.S.S.R. in Asia. Many people suspect that China invaded India in 1962, ostensibly to counteract the Russian propaganda that it "would be the protector of India against aggression from China."[43]

Communism too had to learn about the strength of nationalism in Asia. Sometimes nationalism helped the cause of Communism, as in Vietnam, which always feared Chinese encroachment, Red or otherwise; "a lack of alternatives" kept Vietnam on Moscow Time.[44] On the other hand, the Communist movement of Indonesia was crushed by the combination of nationalism and Islam. More recently, Moscow is not making much headway in nationalistic Afghanistan in spite of its huge investment of money and personnel. In the main, Communism tends to be too ideological to see the realities of Asian revolution. MacMahon Ball suggests that there are three means—military, economic, and psychological—available to the Western Democratic nations in their contest with Communism in Asia. In his view, the importance of the military has been overemphasized. In the economic area, the West oddly enough agrees with the Communist thesis that poverty is the cause of Communism, and the West is determined to pump more technical and economic aid than the U.S.S.R. in order to keep Asia from Communism. MacMahon Ball, without rejecting this assumption altogether, nevertheless does not accept the simple equation of cause and effect between poverty and Communism. "It is not poverty," he insists, "but the *way people come to feel about it* that may create Communists."[45]

Communism, just as Democracy, misunderstands the hidden vitality of Eastern "cultural" and "religious" traditions when it affirms that Communism is based on scientific truth whose complete acceptance alone would deliver Asia from its poverty. (Many Westerners, including Asian specialists, likewise offer their own programs as the only viable solutions to Asia's problems.) Thus far it seems that Communism in Asia took full advantage of the widespread Asian fear of Western colonial imperialism. After all, it did not take much Communist propaganda to convince the illiterate population of Indo-China that Westerners were not fighting the Vietnam War "for Indo-China's independence," as astutely observed by Adlai Stevenson.[46] In so doing, Communism presented itself primarily as a historical force to influence social change, in accordance on the famous Marxist thesis: "The philosophers have only *interpreted* the world, in various ways: the point is, however, to change it."[47] The problem is made more complex by Asia's attempting to form a new religious-cultural-social-political synthesis. And, just as it was impossible to convert Asians completely to the pseudo-religious orientation of secularized salvation during the nineteenth and twentieth centuries, it will be well nigh impossible for Communism to completely alter the thinking of millions of Hindus, Muslims, Buddhists, etc., all accustomed to think of "the return to Totality" as the primordial condition of all existence.

Actually, Communism has some untapped sources if it is willing to use them. For example, in 1923, George Lukács in his *History and Class Consciousness* made it clear that it was not the primacy of economics that differentiates Marxist from other thought but rather "the category of totality, the all-pervasive supremacy of the whole over parts."[48] But unlike Lukács, Communists in Asia have been preoccupied primarily by two things—economics and social change. Sooner or later, however, Communism as much as Democracy will have to confront squarely the "cultural" factor for a more balanced Asian independence. At that level, there will be competition among Western humanistic, scientific, Marxian, Christian as well as traditional or modern Eastern traditions for an explication of the meaning of "totality."

* * * * *

The periods of struggle for political independence and of nation-building were extremely exciting times in Asia. Many things which had been neglected under the Western colonial rule—such as national language, national monuments, national spirit, and traditional social, cultural, and religious institutions—came back into vogue. Gandhi, Nehru, and many other leaders in various parts of Asia relied heavily on the cooperation of traditional religious leaders for the task of creating national unity for the new independent nations.[49] Some of the new Asian governments actively promoted traditional religions. Thus, the immediate post-war Minister for Home and Religions in Burma, after reviewing the British colonial power and ousting of King Thebaw, Promoter of the Faith, stated: "Now the circumstances have changed. Independence is once

more restored. . . . It is but inevitable that the Government become
the Promoter of the Faith, on behalf of the people who elect."[50]
Once revitalized in the heightened emotional atmosphere of
restoration of "tradition," backed enthusiastically by political leaders, the leaders of traditional religions in Asia, began to exert new
energy for (a) the worldly orientation needed for the painstaking
job of nation-building, and (b) world evangelism. Actually, after
political independence was achieved, many political leaders, with
significant exceptions of course, began to suspect that the traditional Eastern religions possess features which are not consonant
with the "more effective symbol creation and symbol manipulation"
needed for social progress.[51]

The "World Evangelism" of traditional Asian religions coincided
with the tide of the increasing influence of the East on Western
cultures and societies, both European and American. It should be
remembered that the East was a novelty before World War II.
There were to be sure some Westerners who knew Asia and were
enthusiastic about some aspects of the Eastern cultures—
eccentrics, professional Orientalists, those who were connected
with Christian world mission, and certain individuals who had lived
in Asia due to business connections. But for the most part, before
the war, Asia was represented in the West as something "far away
and long ago," as someone aptly described it.

The picture changed radically after the war. Already during
World War II many Westerners came to know Asia, either through
fighting in the war, being stationed for other duties after the war,
or meeting war-brides and refugees from Korea and the French-
Indo-China peninsula. But in comparison with the pre-war generations, the West today is much less chauvinistic about its tradition,
and many churches have lost interest in their evangelistic program
abroad. Furthermore, Western education, which until quite recently was preoccupied with the Western tradition, is now willing
to include some Eastern subjects, however minuscule in comparison to the extent to which the West is studied in Asia. Asia has
come into the immediate experience of Westerners today, through
art, movies, flower arrangements, arts of self-defense, transistor ra-

dios, motor cycles, T.V. and automobiles. Moreover, many Westerners are flocking to a variety of Asian religions, not only the well-
established Zen and Vedānta, but many new groups such as Hare
Krishna from India, the Unification Church from Korea, and
Nichiren-shōshū-sōkagakkai from Japan. The increasing Eastern
influence on the West is also seen in the number of Asian intellectuals who are established as teachers, researchers, and technicians
in Western institutions to say nothing of the growing capital in-
vestments into Western societies.

Although increasing Asian influence on the West is not the immediate concern of people in Asia at the moment, it was very much
a part of the background for the future relations between the East
and the West.

The World Has Many Centers

No one but a prophet or a visionary should have the audacity to
speculate about the future of the world. Being neither, let me
quote what I consider a prophetic observation of Adlai Stevenson
who still has something important to say to thoughtful Westerners
in our time:

> Great movements and forces, springing from deep wells, have converged at
> this mid-century point, and I suspect we have barely begun to comprehend
> what has happened and why. In the foreground is the mortal contest with
> world communism. . . . But in the background are the opaque, moving forms
> and shadows of a world revolution, of which communism is more the scav-
> enger than the inspiration; a world in transition from an age with which we
> are familiar to an age shrouded in mist. We . . . have to deal with both the
> foreground and the background of this troubled, anxious age.[52]

This ambiguous situation of world revolution is especially perplex-
ing to the people in Asia who have already experienced a series of
upsetting changes in their social, political, economic, religious, and
cultural life since 1945. Every time I reflect on the complex situation of Asia today, I am reminded of extremely avant-garde sym-
phonic music with its unfamiliar tones and sophisticated instruments. If one's ears have not been specially trained, one does not

know how to comprehend it, for themes are not easily identifiable in such music. Yet, those with attuned ears say that even the most bizarre avant-garde music includes themes, patterns, and structure. Similarly in listening to the bewildering symphony of contemporary Asia, I have been struck by the two motifs—"revolution" and "tradition"—repeated again and again in intricate combinations. Those who have a more static, traditional image of Asia find it difficult to see how revolution is so closely intertwined with tradition. It may be worthwhile, therefore, for us to reflect once again on the nature of the complex Asian situation.

According to MacMahon Ball, the ongoing revolution in Asia has three simultaneous dimensions—(i) a revolt against Western colonialism, (ii) a revolt "against the gross inequalities of fortune," and (iii) "a determination that the destinies of the East will be ends in themselves, not means to Western ends."[53] From an Eastern perspective, the second motif is very striking. Although historically people in Asia have been long-suffering, they no longer accept the fatalistic view which would have been acceptable to their grandparents, that some people were born to be rich and powerful because of merits accumulated in previous existences. Rather, they are now motivated to rectify the "gross inequalities of fortune" with their own efforts here and now. Similarly, many people in Asia are sensitive to the "gross inequalities of fortune" on a global level, between the rich Western nations and the poor nations in Asia and Africa. Hence their determination, both politically and economically, "that the destinies of the East will be ends in themselves, not means to Western ends."

Like all other religions, religions in Asia are grounded in dialectic relationships among three equally fundamental "religious authorities," namely, (a) inherited teachings (scriptures, doctrines and dogmas), (b) traditions (primarily religious but also cultural, social, and political), and (c) the contemporary experience of the people. The radically new contemporary experience of Asia is bound to affect the outlook of religions as a whole, a fact succinctly grasped by a statement made by a Buddhist friend of mine: "for us, history would start tomorrow."

In our speculations on the future of Asia, one of the important factors to be considered is religion. Historically, Asia has been a virtual living museum of diverse religions and quasi-religions. In fact, religions have played decisive roles in shaping cultural and social life in all parts of Asia—Hinduism, Jainism, Sikhism in India; Islam in Pakistan, Afghanistan, Indonesia, Malaya and Bangladesh; Roman Catholic Christianity in the Philippines; Theravāda Buddhism in Southeast Asia; Confucianism, Taoism, and Mahāyāna Buddhism in China; Shinto and Mahāyāna Buddhism in Japan. Of these, with the significant exception of Islam which came originally from the Middle East, most others have historically held "spiritual liberation"—*mokṣa, nirvāṇa, satori*—as the main goal of religious life. Of course, long before Westerners (humanists, liberals, scientists, Christians, Marxists) came to Asia, indigenous religions were attempting to improve the earthly life of their people, fighting against poverty, ignorance, and injustice. But political "freedom" or civil liberty as an essential ingredient for life, individual or corporate, is a new religious agenda in Asia. Thus, one of the crucial questions for Asians today is how to reconcile their inherited belief in "spiritual liberation" as the one soteriological goal with their new affirmation of "freedom" as a necessary precondition for being "fully human" in this world. Many Asians realize that

> When everything has been said and done, it is only a new religious impulse from within the religion concerned that can give the process of reorientation and redirection a new and real vitality. But here we are entering the almost autonomous sphere of personal religious experience. It is, I think, only through the spiritual agony engendered by facing the crisis of the times and through reaching from the depths of one's own religious experience that it becomes possible to reaffirm and restate one's religion's essential relationship with society and to integrate the moral forces impelling the convulsive changes of our time into the living center of one's religion.[54]

Let us now examine very briefly some of the major options that have been proposed in various parts of Asia.

* * * * *

Islam, often still regarded primarily as an Arab religion, is in fact one of the most widespread religions in the world today, claiming roughly one seventh of the total population. Well over 65% of the total Muslim population is found today east of Karachi, Pakistan. For example, Afghanistan, Indonesia and Malaysia have Muslim majorities, while other Asian nations have Muslim minorities. As is well known, Islam from its inception attempted to unite its religious community (*Umma*) within a body-politic. In the words of Muhammad Natsir, the former prime minister of Indonesia: "there exists in Islam no 'church' in the sense of a concrete body having a separate existence within the state. Therefore, Islam cannot conceive of a separation of religion and community, or nation or state."[55] Islam is intensely monotheistic and legalistic, and it tends to uphold the value of the corporate life at the expense of individuals. Kalifa Abdul Hakim goes so far as to say that Muhammad envisioned the creation of a classless society and thus "Islam is theistic socialism."[56] Unfortunately, modern European nations have made beautiful promises to Islamic nations while shamelessly exploiting them. As early as 1906, Czarist Russia sponsored a Muslim conference in Kazan, ostensibly to keep Muslims on the Russian side against the other European nations. Germany established an Islamic society in 1911 for a similar political reason, and Mussolini (who declared he was always right) posed as a defender of Islam, an act which was obviously nothing but a political ploy. Likewise, Hitler promised to save Muslims from the aggression of the Jews whom he called a "counter-race" (*Gegenreich*). The record of Western so-called "democratic" nations' relations with Islamic nations is notoriously poor. Muslims were shocked by Winston Churchill's reckless proposal "to partition Persia between Britain and Russia to save the properties of an oil company."[57] No wonder Abdul Qayyum writes: "The pattern has been the same; each of the Great Powers has sought to exploit Moslem credulity to suit its own strategic plans."[58]

Understandably, Islamic nations in Asia no longer trust their destinies to Western colonial nations. And, since the end of World War II, Asian Muslims have experimented with various combinations of "revolutionary" and "traditional" thrusts in order to blend "spiritual liberation" and "human freedom" in today's world. The emergence of a self-conscious Muslim state called Pakistan introduced a brand new element in Asia after World War II. Pakistan came into existence, as Charles J. Adams rightly points out, as the result of a religious group in the Indian subcontinent awakening to political self-consciousness. To Pakistanis, it was not enough to achieve political independence. Their state must become a religiously inspired state, as asserted in the Objective Resolution in 1949: "Wherein the Muslims shall be enabled to order their lives in the individual and collective spheres in accord with the teachings and requirements of Islam as set out in the Holy Qur'ān and the Sunna (Tradition)." In so stating, Pakistanis reaffirmed the historical Islamic principle of spiritual democracy as the only viable option for Muslims in the modern world. Clearly the architects of Pakistan "were not seeking solely to build their own ideal society but to hold out to all men a model from which they might profit."[59] After the initial enthusiasm however, it became evident that Islam's past provided little help to the Pakistanis for meeting modern problems (as evidenced by a series of upheavals, including the establishment of another independent Muslim state, Bangladesh, out of the Eastern wing of Pakistan in 1971 and the execution of former prime minister, Zulfikae Ali Bhutto, followed by a blatant form of military dictatorship). Now the whole world is watching how Pakistan will be guided by Bhutto's daughter, the new prime minister.

Approximately 35 million Muslims remained in India rather than moving to Pakistan at the time when the Indian peninsula was divided in 1947, and they have been determined to lead their lives as both Indians and Muslims. Although faithfully accepting the Qur'ān and the Traditions, Indian-Muslims interpret them in the light of their actual experience in a non-Muslim Indian state. The Islamic tradition in India, especially in the Bengal area, has always stressed the importance of vernacular Islam on the grounds that "only if Islamic values and cultural images were expressed in the regional languages would human beings with a nature greatly removed from that in the Arabic- and Persian-speaking lands be able to make the Islamic perception of reality both meaningful and their own."[60] In this respect, Muslims in India share both problems and promises with Muslim minorities in other Asian nations such as Singapore, the Philippines, and Thailand.[61] Muslims in India, like other citizens, enjoy the state's constitutional guarantee of freedom of religion for their religious institutions. The question still remains, however, as to how much religious law, in addition to the secular code, is required for Muslims to preserve their religious belief. The basic problems confronting Islam in India and other non-Muslim nations today are succinctly summarised by Federspiel as follows:

1. State leaders seek to create a code of civic values as the supreme value system within the state to which all citizens and communal groups must adhere. . . .

2. *State leaders seek to circumscribe the political activities of Muslim leaders and prevent Muslims from challenging their authority over the state.* . . .

3. Muslim leaders seek to place Islamic principles in effect . . . [as] the basis for any civic culture erected by the nation for its entire population. . . .[62]

Muslims in Indonesia face a situation different from that of Muslims in Pakistan, or that of those in other countries where Muslims are considered minority groups. Even though 80 percent of its total population belongs to the Islamic faith, Indonesia gained political independence as a "national" rather than as a "Muslim" state, according to Sukarno, the first president.

(Indonesia proclaimed its independence in 1945, but the Netherlands did not transfer sovereignty until 1949.) The guiding ideologues of the Indonesian Republic have been called the "Five Principles"—belief in the divine One, humanity, nationalism, democracy and social justice. Indonesian Muslims are trying to reconcile the sacred law of Islam with pre-Islamic local customs and practices. The government has a Ministry of Religion which coordinates and controls all religious activities of the republic, following "a middle course between the theory of complete separation of religion and the state and the theory of unity of religion and state."[63]   One of the most active post-war organizations in Indonesia has been Bajankara Islam, which promotes religious education of the populace with the moral backing of the central government. There are of course fanatic Islamic groups which agitate for the establishment of a Muslim state, and there has been a sizable group of communist sympathizers whose activities precipitated a *coup d'état* which put General Suharto in power in 1965. President Sukarno was forced to accept a new military-civilian government handpicked by Suharto. (Suharto became the president in 1968.)

Muslims in Pakistan, India, and Indonesia propose different ways of mixing revolutionary and traditional impulses to attain the twin objectives of "spiritual liberation" and "human freedom." These Asian Muslims represent a significant portion of the world-wide Islamic community, which in turn constitutes a powerful block in world affairs as dramatically demonstrated in oil diplomacy, the Islamic Foreign Ministers' Conference, the World Islam League, and the Voice of Islam radio station in Germany. In all this, we have to remember that Islam is not a monolithic system, as many uninformed observes often claim.   Islam has its share of conservatives, fundamentalists, modernists, and even secularists. But, as Noel Coulson astutely observes, the problem facing Islam in Asia today is "inherent in its nature—the need to define the relationship between the standards imposed by the religious faith and the mundane forces that activate society."[64]

* * * * *

Every time I visit India it confirms someone's impression stated many years ago that there was no simple explanations for what is happening to Hinduism or the state of India—both Hinduism and India are very ancient and very young. The familiar portrait of Mahatma Gandhi reminds us of India's persistent struggle to reconcile its "traditions" with "revolutionary" forces. There is much truth in Kraemer's observation that Hinduism has never abandoned the "magical circle of the innate assumption that man is essentially one with all the other parts of Nature."[65] Hinduism has been integrally related to the "natural" institutions of the family, the village, and above all the caste system, which is both a system of social stratification and a cosmological hierarchy. Obviously, throughout the long history of India, Hindus tended to equate the "natural" with the "traditional"—thinking, cults, customs, and habits. The resurgence of modern Hinduism started as a "reform" movement in the nineteenth century. It was a "reform" in the sense that the "natural" was to be emancipated from the "traditional," particularly those customs which the reformers considered undesirable, such as caste restrictions in social intercourse, enforced widowhood and other restrictions for women, the treatment of the "untouchables," and the rigidity of the joint-family system. Some reformers have tried to modify the traditional teachings and practices of Hinduism in the light of what they considered natural. Some were persuaded that the best form of the natural is classical Hinduism. Still others rejected the traditional altogether, and with it the classical foundation of Hinduism itself. And many reformers combined different approaches.

Any discussion of modern Hinduism or the state of India cannot overlook the enormous influence of Mahatma Gandhi. As John Gunther puts it, Gandhi represented "an incredible combination of Jesus Christ, Tammany Hall, and your father."[66]

Gandhi's programs were multi-dimensional and his achievements were many. Among them, his life-long work for the improvement of India's villages, for Hindu-Muslim unity, and for the abolition of untouchability will long be remembered. He insisted that spiritual values were the basis of his social, economic, and political programs. To him, India's political independence was hardly the end in itself. Chester Bowls tells us that on Independence Day, August 15, 1947, while India was celebrating its political freedom from British rule, "Gandhi was on a third-class railway coach, heading for the riot area of Bengal where he spent the day in mourning, fasting, prayer, and spinning."[67] Gandhi's influence was far from negligible in making Hinduism a living, spiritual force. But he was not against the West. He clearly saw the future of Hinduism, India and Asia "not for Asia but for the whole world."[68] Sadly, as Schilp observed, "Hindus by the millions now are discovering what Christians have found over nineteen centuries: 'It is infinitely easier to worship an ideal than to live by it.' "[69] Gandhi's name has been invoked by the Left Wing, by the Right Wing, and by the Congress Party, which from the time of Pandit Nehru, through his daughter, Indira Gandhi (her husband was not related to Mahatma), and under the leadership of her son, Rajiv Gandhi, has been trying to take the difficult middle of the road.[70]

The Republic of India is attempting to establish a "secular state," not too different from eighteenth-century America, where the principle of religious liberty was hammered out. This principle has been supported by a majority of the Hindus as well as by the religious minorities, including Neo-Buddhists and Christians, but it is sharply attacked by the Right Wing Hindus who want to make India a "Hindu state." Despite the constitutional guarantee of religious freedom, Hinduism exerts a tremendous influence on all spheres of contemporary India. And Hinduism now tries to utilize both revolutionary and traditional impulses to relate "spiritual liberation" and "human freedom." Concretely, according to Devanandan, today the Hindus desire: (i) to relate science and religion, (ii) to integrate the dynamics of secularism, (iii) to redefine the classical Hindu view of the "divine" nature of human beings in light of the modern scientific theory of evolution, and (iv) to re-integrate the cultural values of classical Hinduism into contemporary life.[71] Meanwhile, contemporary Indian society faces tough prob-

lems, like the political aspirations of Muslims, Sikhs, and other minority groups, relations with neighborhood nations, and continued
poverty and over-population. Especially crucial is the financial
foundation of Indian society. Shortly after World War II, Nehru
commented that "India's liberal constitution will only last if the Indian economic plan can engender a sense of economic progress at
least equal to that of China."[72] Today, India faces a crisis which is
as devastating as it was in Nehru's time.[73] It is hoped, however,
that Hindus today will not forget the important legacy of Gandhi
who believed that social, economic, and political issues cannot be
divorced from the spiritual.

* * * * *

There are many different perspectives from which one can approach Buddhism. For example, many Hindu scholars, as well as
the Western scholars they influenced, consider Buddhism an offshoot of Hinduism and refer to it as one of the heterodox systems
in India. Others see it as the expression of a unique religious experience, different from that of historical Brahmanic-Hinduism,
though Buddhism appropriated many of the Hindu symbols and
rhetoric in communicating its faith to people in Indian society and
culture. Historically, Buddhism was a pan-Asian religion, and it has
become self-consciously a world-wide faith in our century. As a
pan-Asian religion, Buddhism developed three "secondary centers
of diffusion"—(i) Ceylon (Sri Lanka) for Southern Buddhism,
which spread through South and Southeast Asia and is often referred to as Hinayāna (Small Vehicle) or Theravāda (Tradition of
the Elders); (ii) China for northern Buddhism, commonly called
Mahāyāna (Great Vehicle), which is found in China, Korea and
Japan; and (iii) Tibet for the esoteric branch known as Vajrayāna
or Mantrayāna, which became the faith of the Tibetans and the
Mongols. In this section, our primary concern is Southern Buddhism, which became the national faith of states in South and
Southeast Asia. (Esoteric Buddhism is becoming popular in the
West, but we still know very little about the Esoteric Buddhism sit-

uation in Tibet and Mongolia except for information from the
Dalai Lama's group in India. For the most part, Mahāyāna Buddhism did not replace other religions but "supplemented" indigenous traditions in China and Japan.)

The renewed vitality of Southern Buddhism was accelerated by
the heightened national consciousness of South and Southeast
Asian nations in their struggle to be emancipated from European
control. For example, in 1950, the Burmese government established the Union Buddha Sāsana Council for the renovation of
pagodas and for the propagation of Buddhism. Today, for the first
time in the 2500 years of Buddhist history, the various traditions of
Buddhism are discovering each other, as evidenced by the formation of the World Fellowship of Buddhists, which has been meeting
every two or three years since 1950 in various nations. Moreover,
the Buddhist community is not essentially a national or even a regional, but a world-wide community. Not only is Buddhism no
longer defensive, as it was earlier in our century, but many Buddhists are persuaded that Buddhism alone can fulfill all the objectives of religion and civilization. Thus U Chan Htoon, at one time
Burma's Attorney-General, declared in 1950:

> Buddhism is the *only* ideology which can give peace to the world and save it
> from war and destruction. I found there that the western countries are
> longing for Buddhism now. What is the cause of it? They find in Buddhism
> the real truth which can save man from the endless sorrow and suffering into
> which they have been plunged by following ideologies which they have now
> found out to be false and inadequate. . . . For that reason *the people of the
> world are looking up to Buddhism to save the world.*"[74]

By far the most epoch-making even in the post-war history of Buddhism was the Sixth Buddhist Council, held in Rangoon, Burma
from 1954 to 1956. This gigantic undertaking was engineered to a
great extent by U Nu, then the prime minister, whom many
Burmese thought of as the ideal Buddhist ruler. He was said to
seek "the re-sacralizing of the government as significantly advancing Burma along the road either to a Lokka Nibban ["perfect
world"] . . . or . . . into greater readiness for the Maitreya Buddha,

the coming Buddha, in whose near advent some Burmese believe."[75] This does not mean U Nu was simply to restore historical Buddhism. One has to understand what Sarkisyanz calls "U Nu's particular conciliation of tradition and revolution"[76] in order to appreciate his brand of modern Buddhism, an unusual combination of Buddhism with insights taken from Fabianism, Marxism, Socialism, and the welfare state. At any rate, largely through his initiative, the Constitutional amendment passed in 1961 made Buddhism the state religion of Burma. In 1961 the President of the Union of Burma declared that "Burma can be developed into a prosperous, democratic, modern welfare state, only if it is based upon three factors, viz., nationalism, scientific technology, and Buddhism."[77] Similar rhetoric on the Buddhist welfare state was uttered by the now deposed Prince Sihanouk of Cambodia and the leaders of Sri Lanka, Laos, and Vietnam. Some leaders even advocated collaboration with Communism on the ground that "Marxist theory refers to worldly affairs and seeks to satisfy material needs [while] Buddhist philosophy . . . deals with spiritual things, with the liberation from this world."[78]

Buddhists in subsequent years found it exceedingly difficult to reconcile the soteriological aim of attaining Nirvana (Nibbana) with the socio-economic and political aims of a social welfare state, based on the principles of liberty, freedom, justice, equality and welfare. Some critics even question the ability of committed Buddhists, who hold that the things of this world are worthless, to function effectively in today's Asia. Moreover, recent trends indicate that Buddhism is confronted by mild antagonism from the ruling regimes of Sri Lanka and Burma and open hostility from the Communist regimes in Vietnam, Laos, and Cambodia. It is impossible to estimate how many Buddhist leaders, clerical and lay, have been sentenced to reeducation camps in the Indo-China peninsula. The situation is probably the worst in Cambodia (Kampuchea), where Buddhism is considered a reactionary religion and treated as such. On the other hand, there are many new and creative attempts at blending spiritual liberation and human freedom in various parts of Asia—from among the Neo-Buddhists (mostly former harijans or outcastes) in India to a variety of newly created lay Buddhist groups in Japan. But as yet there is no generally agreed upon formula for harnessing revolutionary and traditional thrusts for the creation of a religious-cultural-social-political synthesis.

*   *   *   *   *

Although in this volume we have dealt primarily with the nations and people who gained independence from the yoke of European colonialism after World War II in South and Southeast Asia, we might also give a cursory look at East Asia, which took a very different course after 1945. First, following the war, Japan was until 1952 ruled by the Supreme Commander of the Allied Occupation Forces (SCAP). With Japan's defeat, Korea (which was soon split between the Communist North and the anti-Communist South) and Formosa (Taiwan) were emancipated from Japanese colonial rule. The Chinese Communists under the leadership of Mao Tse-tung defeated Chiang Kai-shek's Kuomintang regime and established the People's Republic of China in 1949 in the mainland, while Chiang Kai-shek and his followers resettled in Formosa which then became the headquarters of his Republic of China. In 1950, the Korean War broke out between the Democratic People's Republic of Korea (North) and the Republic of Korea (South), and by the time of the armistice in 1952, that war had involved the U.S. based United Nations forces and 180,000 Chinese "volunteers." It is estimated that altogether about 5,000,000 lives were lost during the conflict. Obviously, all these developments greatly changed the lives of the people in East Asia. Through it all the tension between "revolution" and "tradition" had been keenly felt.

As for modern religious developments in Japan,[79] starting in 1868 the Meiji government restored the ancient principle of the unity of religion and government (*saisei-itchi*) but at the same time welcomed the introduction of Western thought, technology, and civilization in general. Curiously, the Meiji government encour-

aged on the one hand popular rights (*minken*) and religious freedom of a sort, while on the other hand it created State Shinto and
advocated the emperor cult as a non-religious patriotic duty for all
Japanese subjects.   One can readily see, therefore, that the dises-
tablishment of State Shinto by the Allied Occupation forces in
1945 together with the newly declared principle of genuine religious freedom (the axiom of the separation of religion and state)
and the emperor's own public denial of the divinity of the throne
had far-reaching implications.   The Occupation forces prohibited
the sponsorship, support, perpetuation, control, and dissemination
of State Shinto by any branch of the Japanese government.   Thus
assured of religious freedom, the Buddhist, Christian, and Sect
Shinto denominations now vigorously carry on their multiple activities.   Nevertheless, there is a widespread feeling among the populace that they have lost the core of their spiritual heritage, according to which Japan was not only their native country but a sacred
land hallowed by the presence of *kami* ("the sacred").   It was assumed historically that the meaning of human existence was integrally related to the well-being of the divine land and the sacred national community.[80]   This may account for the popularity of the
new religions primarily as "crisis religions," although the real
growth of these religions came after the Korean War, which
marked the beginning of the period of affluency in Japan.   Blending ethnocentrism, folk religious ethos, and modern techniques of
communication and organizational skill, these new religions claim
to provide a coherent meaning of life, which—according to
them—is not readily given by such traditional religious traditions as
Shinto, Buddhism, and Christianity.   Millions of Japanese people
miss the sense of belonging in the highly competitive and dehu-
manized new Japan.   What is especially appealing is the
"horizontal" social structure of the new religions in the "vertically
structured" Japanese society.[81]   The questions which haunts all religious leaders today is whether or not Japan, a secular nation-state
with highly advanced science, technology and industry, can leave
room for a yearning for "spiritual liberation."

Space unfortunately does not allow us to discuss the highly explosive situation in Korea.[82] We can ill afford, however, to ignore China.

"The Chinese," so wrote John Gunther, "possess the largest country and longest civilization known to mankind. They have uninterruptedly existed as a political and cultural entity for well over 4,000 years, a record no country in the world can match. The Chinese were old when ancient Greece was young; they produced Confucius centuries before Alexander the Great or Julius Caesar; they were having a magnificently mature development when Europe was a medieval shambles."[83] Although no one Western nation had colonial power over China in the nineteenth and twentieth centuries, many European nations, the U.S., and Japan jointly and individually exploited China. But, when Sun Yat-sen's revolution toppled the Manchu dynasty in 1912 and the republic really needed outside help, "the western powers would have nothing to do with this struggling revolution—which, indeed, they opposed bitterly. The British, the French [and others] were not too friendlily disposed to a national movement which might end their own privileges."[84] In 1928, conservative Chiang Kai-shek maneuvered to gain leadership of Sun's party, the Kuomintang. During the 1930's and World War II, China was under constant threat from Japanese militarists, but Chiang and his regime were not fully responsive to the peoples' desire for the united front to resist Japanese attacks. Meanwhile, the Chinese Communist party under Mao Tse-tung skillfully took advantage of the situation and drove Chiang and his followers to Taiwan in 1949.[85]

One is bound to be struck by the uniqueness of the Chinese Communists' synthesis of "tradition" and "revolution." In a sense Maoism, which claimed to bring about a "new culture," was the continuation of the traditional Chinese culture but with a radical reinterpretation based on the guiding principles of Marx and Lenin. The characteristic of Mao Tse-tung's thought was the two-pronged attitude of saying "no but yes" to Chinese tradition while saying "yes but no" to Marx-and-Lenin. Unlike the traditional Chinese who looked for the paradigmatic meaning of history in the legendary golden period of the ancient sage kings, Mao shifted the locus of the meaning of history from the past to the present and future. Thus, past historical events were judged not by whether they conformed to the ancient moral norm, but whether their meaning could be profitably utilized to give impetus to the creation of a new form of culture yet to emerge in China. In his numerous writings, Mao made it clear that his heroes were not the ancient sage kings nor the proletariat (as the Soviet-oriented Communists expected), but rather the peasant masses who actualized the new culture in China. Indeed, the revolution under Mao's leadership during his lifetime, with the exception of his last years, was a great success. From 1956, with the increasing rift in Sino-Soviet relations, Peking began to assert itself as *the* major power which singlehandedly could redeem the whole world from the evils of Soviet revisionism and American capitalism (quite a switch from Sun Yat-sen's dream of synthesizing the Soviet and American systems).[86] In this messianic role, Peking universalized its own synthesis of "tradition" and "revolution" as a model for other nations in the Third World.[87] In the eyes of other oppressed nations, however, this image of a messianic China was marred by Peking's admission to the U.N. and her rapprochement with the U.S. In addition, the great Proletarian Cultural Revolution which Mao instigated in 1966 proved to be as great a disaster as his earlier program of industrialization, the Great Leap Forward of 1958-61.

With Mao's death in 1976, China closed one page of revolution and turned another page of revolutionary change under the leadership of Deng Xiaoping, who repudiated many of Mao's policies. Deng and the new regime are careful not to hold Mao (and indirectly themselves) responsible for all the major errors of recent decades and choose to blame the "Gang of Four," which includes Mao's widow, for all the errors and crimes. Yet, Deng's new synthesis of "revolution" and "tradition," necessarily including some of Mao's legacy, while restoring free-market incentives, may not be able to keep the people's desire for the promised political reforms from surfacing for very long.[88]

* * * * *

Before concluding our brief survey, it might be appropriate to add a short footnote on "Christianity," not one of the traditionally Asian religions and as such usually excluded from discussions of the religious situation in modern Asia. In reality, however, Christianity has had a long history in Asia, as exemplified by Syrian Christian groups in South India who trace their origin to the legendary visit of St. Thomas; by Nestorian Christian groups during the T'ang period (A.D. 618-907); by Nestorian and Roman Catholic friar activities in China under the Mongol rule (thirteenth and fourteenth centuries); and by the Portuguese and Spanish missionary enterprises in various parts of Asia, with such notable figures as Francis Xavier (d. 1552), nicknamed a *conquistador* of souls in Asia, Matteo Ricci (d. 1610), the priest-scientist in China, and Robert de Nobili (d. 1656), the missionary-Sannyāsin in India. Probably the most tangible legacy of the Roman Catholic missionary work in Asia is the large Catholic population in the Philippines, which constitutes approximately 85 percent of all Filipinos. In addition, there are the Protestant missionary societies, which had extensive evangelistic, educational, and philanthropic programs in various parts of Asia during the nineteenth and twentieth centuries. According to a contemporary missiologist, some of the weaknesses of Christianity in Asia can be accounted for historically—"in many cases by reason of a long period of missionary tutelage, a too-great dependence on missionary society leadership and finance, a limited understanding of the gospel in pietistic and individualistic terms, and a view of the church distorted by the divided nature of Western [Christianity]."[89]

In the main, Christian groups in Asia—both Catholic and Protestant—are sharply divided into two groups: a larger number of adherents among the lower strata of society, partly because it was much easier for statistics-conscious missionaries to convert them, and a very small number of faithful among the urban intelligentsia, with very few in between. Thus, in a place like Japan, where church activities were aimed at well-educated populations in cities,

Christians are numerically very small. And some of the adherents who almost "converted themselves" (according to the Neo-Confucian principle that truth is one, for instance) baffled many Western missionaries.[90] It was Uchimura's conviction not to depend on Western missionaries that resulted in his so-called "non-church church."[91] It is a matter of some significance that the small Japanese Christian community produced such a figure as Toyohiko Kagawa, who had an abiding faith that Christian witness must at the same time find articulate expression in the social, economic, educational, and political dimensions of life.[92]

Asian Christians are rightly proud of the fact that the Church of South India, the first successful union—since the Reformation—of episcopal and non-episcopal groups, came into existence in 1947, thus beginning a new page in Christian history. Christian groups in India enthusiastically support the emerging Indian principle of a "secular state," which of course does not reject a deeply spiritual society; I am persuaded that some principle of this sort will be the most realistic and defensible one for the future world. Indian Christians are in a good position to persuade not only fellow Christians but other religious groups that each tradition must be able to pursue its religious goal and yet must be able to cohabit with other religious traditions peacefully with a sense of mutual trust and mutual respect.

Christian groups in China are also trying to adjust to the difficult social, economic, and political situation today. Much has been written on the "Three-Self Movement"—self-support, self-government, and self-propagation—of the Protestant groups and the Chinese Catholic Patriotic Association (CCPA). One can understand the critique of these groups by many Westerners. Many orthodox Western Roman Catholics are particularly bothered that CCPA does not pay allegiance to Rome. But critics do not see the positive aspects of the Three-Self movement and of CCPA. Both Protestant and Catholic forms of Christianity are somehow surviving in China under trying circumstances.[93]

Those who followed the events of the bloodless revolution in the Philippines in February, 1986 are of course aware of the strong support given to the movement headed by Corazon Aquino by the Roman Catholic hierarchy. Outsiders should not hastily conclude that this was an opportunity for the Roman Catholic Church simply to have its political muscle felt in the Philippines. Both clerical and lay leaders of the Filipino church are engaged in a serious re-assessment of the Christian responsibility to society and culture. As early as 1965, one senator was deeply concerned with the fact that "the fate-dominated and consumption-oriented mentality of the Filipino is an integral part of his essentially Asian culture, and the fact that this mentality remains strong today is due to Hispanic Catholicism's compromise with that culture rather than to the inner nature of Catholicism itself."[94] This kind of stance, however, begs the larger question of the relationship between Christianity and Asian religious-cultural traditions, not only in the Philippines but in other parts of Asia too.

Concern for the much used concept of *Anknuepfungspunkt* ("point of contact") between Christianity and Asian traditions has resulted in our time in the establishment of Christian centers for the study of indigenous religions, cultures, and societies in many key spots in Asia: Bangalore, India; Colombo, Sri Lanka; Hong Kong; and Kyoto and Nagoya, Japan.[95] Many Christians are now stressing the importance of "dialogue" between Christianity and Asian religions.[96]

Moreover, now that many Asian nations have emerged from the colonial phase, many Asian-born Christian theologians (both Catholic and Protestant)—without rejecting the path of "dialogue," to be sure—are trying to articulate Christian theologies in the light of their living experience. One significant concept which has come to be used frequently is "contextual theology." According to the statement by the Theological Education Fund (now the Programme of Theological Education): "Contextualization has to do with how we assess the peculiarity of Third World contexts. Indigenization tends to be used in the sense of responding to the [Christian] Gospel in terms of a *traditional culture*. Contextualiza-tion, while not ignoring this, takes into account the process of sec-ularity, technology, and the struggle for human justice, which characterize the *historical moment* of nations of the Third World."[97] In so stating, advocates of "contextual theology" have to face the intricate relations between "text" (Christian Gospel) and "context" (Contemporary Third World), much as the global Christian movement of "Faith and Order" faces many alternative approaches, e.g., "Faith is Order," "Faith versus Order," "Faith of Order," "Order of Faith," "Faith and Order in Dialogue," etc. Clearly, Christianity in Asia, too, has to take seriously the reality of the "revolutionary" and "traditional" thrust of the contemporary Third World in order to show the dialectical relationship between spiritual liberation and human freedom in today's Asia.

*　*　*　*　*

Even such a brief and rather superficial sketch of contemporary Asia as I have attempted makes it clear that Asians are now struggling to harness "traditional" and "revolutionary" drives in order to bring about a viable future. It is sobering to think that between now and the year 2000 (which is around the corner) the map of Asia, like the map of the rest of the world, might be redrawn several times. It would be a mistake to think of the future of Asia primarily in terms of power politics and foreign relations. We must be sensitive to the internal struggle of Asian people to reconcile their received faiths in spiritual liberation with their newly awakened sense of human freedom. It must be recognized that in contemporary Asia, as elsewhere, freedom refers to the human effort to be emancipated from something, such as the established order of society, an outmoded standard of morality, an archaic system of religious doctrines, or hunger and material need. On the other hand, freedom also refers to our aspirations for novelty and creativity in art, philosophy, religion, and interhuman relations. The all-important question for Asians is how to develop a creative linkage between the ultimate end of human existence and the empirical need for freedom. In this situation, religions in Asia carry a heavy burden as they try to relate the still creative resources of "tradition" and the purifying, transforming dynamics of the "revolutionary" impulse.

Neither a prophet nor a visionary, I cannot discern the future of Asia. I do sense, however, the one important question which haunts all Asians who have been touched by the revolutionary changes in contemporary Asia. "The question is whether in the end the man of the East will have lost himself, whether he will be hopelessly subservient to the spirit of the West or whether he will emerge from the encounter a new man, who has found the way to a peculiar, creative reshaping of his life, as a nation and as a person."[98] Unfortunately, as Carlos Romulo, former President of the University of the Philippines, pointed out, for too long the West has viewed Asia simply as a scene, arena, or landscape for the West to play out its historical roles. But, "the world may well know that Asia has ceased to be a mere stage, for it is the world which is the stage and all must play their individual roles."[99] Asian proposals—whether from Hindus, Buddhists, Muslims or Asian Christians—for relating spiritual liberation and human freedom may not be wholly appealing, but those proposals are the fruit of long and painful encounters with history. And in the kind of world in which we are destined to live today there is room for more than one coherent view of life and the world. All of us, Easterners and Westerners alike, will have to realize sooner or later, as Thomas Mann's Joseph realized in Egypt, that "the world has many centers."

Notes

1 See Gunnar Myrdal, *Asian Drama: An Inquiry into the Poverty of Nations* (3 vols.; New York: Pantheon, 1968) I, 73 and 103.

2 See J.M. Kitagawa, *The 1893 World's Parliament of Religions and Its Legacy* (Chicago: The University of Chicago—The Divinity School 1984), 5.

3 H.J. Morgenthau, *In Defense of the National Interest* (New York: A.A. Knopf, 1951), 60.

4 Tu Ting-hsiu; Quoted in H.F. MacNair, ed., *China*, trans. Tu Ting-hsiu (Berkeley: University of California Press, 1946), xxxv.

5 Z.N. Zeine, *Arab-Turkish Relations and the Emergence of Arab Nationalism* (Beirut: Khayat, 1958), 125.

6 H.A.R. Gibb, "Near Eastern Perspective: The Present and the Future," in *Near Eastern Culture and Society*, ed. by T.C. Young (Princeton: Princeton University Press, 1951), 230.

7 Panikkar, *Asia and Western Dominance*, 195.

8 For a popular account of Gandhi's activities before World War II, see John Gunther, *Inside Asia* (New York: Harper, 1939), 334-369.

9 J. Nehru, *The Discovery of India* (New York: John Day, 1956), 579.

10 Dean, *The Nature of the Non-Western World*, 113.

11 G.B. Sansom, *The Western World and Japan* (New York: A.A. Knopf, 1962), 407.

12 See J.M. Kitagawa and F.E. Reynolds, "Theravada Buddhism in the Twentieth Century," in H. Dumoulin and J.C. Maraldo, eds., *Buddhism in the Modern World* (New York: Macmillan, 1976), 52.

13 *Ibid.*, 53.

14 Dean, *Non-Western World*, 141-142.

15 Panikkar, *Western Dominance*, 191.

16 Konvitz, *The Alien and the Asiatic in American Law*, 26.

17 *Ibid.*, 23.

18 Irving Kristol, "The 20th Century Began in 1945," *New York Times Magazine*, May 2, 1965, 25.

19 J. Nehru, *Jawaharal Nehru's Speeches* (New Delhi: Government of India, Publication Division, 1949), 25.

20 For a good general account of the "Bandung Conference," read K.M. Panikkar's and C.P. Fitzgerald's views in *The Nation*, 180:14 (April 2, 1955), 287-289.

21 W. MacMahon Ball, *Nationalism and Communism in East Asia* (Melbourne: University Press, 1952), 149.

22 A.J. Toynbee, "The Outlook for the West Today," *Motive*, December, 1961, 14.

23 A.J. Toynbee, *The World and the West* (New York: Oxford University Press, 1953), 13-14.

24 Morgenthau, *In Defense*, 63.

25 Ball, *Nationalism and Communism*, 2.

26 H.R. Isaacs, "The Dimension of the Crisis," *Saturday Review of Literature*, XXXIV, 31 (August 4, 1951), 13.

27 N. Mansergh, "The Impact of Asian Membership," *The Listener*, December 8, 1954, 1001.

28 Paul Devanandan and M.M. Thomas, eds., *Communism and Social Revolution in India* (Calcutta: YMCA, 1953), 7.

29 Morgenthau, *In Defense*, 201.

30 A.J. Toynbee, *Civilization on Trial* (New York: Oxford University Press, 1948), 83.

31 Panikkar and Fitzgerald, the "Bandung Conference," 288.

32 See Vernon Bartlett, "Opening of Bandung Conference," *Manchester Guardian*, Air Edition, April 21, 1955.

33 F.S.C. Northrop, *The Taming of the Nations* (New York: Macmillan, 1952), 67.

34 Panikkar and Fitzgerald, the "Bandung Conference," 287.

35 W.L. Mackenzie King quoted in the *Chicago Sun-Times*, Saturday, January 3, 1976.

36 C.P. Romulo, "A Policy for the West in Asia," *Saturday Review of Literature*, XXXIX, 31 (August 4, 1951), 11; emphasis added.

37 See, for example, J.K. Fairbank, ed., *The Missionary Enterprise in China and America* (Cambridge: Harvard University PRess, 1974).

38 W.W. Rostow, with R.W. Hatch, *An American Policy in Asia* (New York: John Wiley, 1955), 4.

39 Adlai Stevenson quoted in the *Chicago Sun-Times*, September 18, 1953, 14.

40 Isaacs, "The Dimension," 14.

41 See Ajit Roy, "A Marxist View of Liberation," in S.J. Samartha, ed., *Living Faiths and Ultimate Goals* (Geneva: W.C.C., 1974), 56-67.

42 Morgenthau, *In Defense*, 205.

43 See Walter Lippman, "Our Involvement in Asia's Crisis," *Chicago Sun-Times*, November 1, 1962, 44.

44 *The Reporter*, January 27, 1955, 13.

45 Ball, *Nationalism and Communism*, 198; emphasis added.

46 Stevenson, in the *Chicago Sun-Times*, September 18, 1953, 16.

47 Quoted in Roy, "A Marxist View," 60.

48 See Martin Jay, *Marxism and Totality* (Berkeley: University of California Press, 1974), 81-127.

49 See, for example, E. Sarkisyanz, *Buddhist Background of the Burmese Revolution* (The Hague: Martinus Nijhoff, 1965).

50 Quoted in G.P. Charles, "Let God Speak," *Burma Christian Council Annual* (Rangoon, 1953), 27-28.

51 See Soedjatmoko, "Cultural Motivations to Progress: the 'Exterior' and the 'Interior Views'," in R.N. Bellah, ed., *Religion and Progress in Modern Asia* (New York: The Free Press, 1965), 1-14.

52 A. Stevenson, *Call to Greatness* (New York: Harper, 1954), 1.

53 Ball, *Nationalism and Communism*, 2.

54 Soedjatmoko, "Cultural Motivations," 8.

55 Quoted in R.B. Manikam, ed., *Christianity and the Asian Revolution* (New York: Friendship Press, 1954), 153.

56 K.A. Hakim, "One God, One Word, One Humanity," in Anshen, *Moral Principles of Action*, 597.

57 See R.E. Turner, "The Nature of the Crisis," *Saturday Review of Literature*, XXXIV, 31 (August 4, 1951), 16.

58 A. Qayyaum, "The Role of Islam in Asia," *Saturday Review of Literature*, ibid., 37.

59 Charles J. Adams, "Islam in Pakistan," in J.M. Kitagawa, ed., *Modern Trends in World Religions* (La Salle, IL: Open Court, 1959), I have used his article freely in this section.

60 P. Hardy, "Islam in South Asia," Eliade, *The Encyclopedia of Religion*, VII, 397-398.

61 See H.M. Federspiel, "Islam and Development in the Nations of ASEAN, *Asian Survey*, Vol. XXV, No. 8 (August 1945); 805-821.

62 *Ibid.*, 815.

63 Manikam, *Christianity*, 167-168.

64 See N.J. Coulson, "The Concept of Progress and Islamic Law," Bellah, *Religion and Progress*, 89.

65 Kraemer, *World Cultures*, 11.

66 J. Gunther, *Inside Asia*, 344.

67 C. Bowles, *Ambassador's Report* (New York: Harper, 1954), 70.

68 *Ibid.*, 68.

69 P.A. Schilp, "Some Call Him God. . .Gandhi in Retrospect," *Chicago Sun-Times*, February 16, 1958.

70 In the light of what has happened to India in recent decades, it is extremely interesting to reread Norman Cousin's article, "Talk with the PM," *Saturday Review*, May 27, 1961, 10-33, subtitled "Nehru: My Legacy to India. Hopefully, It is 400,000,000 People Capable of Governing Themselves."

71 Quoted in Manikam, *Christianity*, 137.

72 J. Nehru's statement reported in the *Manchester Guardian*, December 23, 1954.

73 See J.A. Bernard, "A Maturation Crisis in India: The V.P. Singh Experiment," *Asian Survey*, XXVII, No. 4 (April 1987), 408-426.

74 Quoted in Sarkisyanz, *Buddhist Background*, 204.

75 *Ibid.*, 209.

76 *Ibid.*, 217.

77 Quoted from the statement of President U Win Maung, read at the Sixth Conference of Buddhists (Autumn 1961, at Phnom Penh, Cambodia).

78 Quoted in Ernst Benz, *Buddhism or Communism: Which Holds the Future of Asia?* (New York: Doubleday, 1965), 227.

79 Those who are especially interested in this matter should be referred to Kitagawa, *On Understanding Japanese Religion*, Chapter 16, "The Religious Ethos of Present-Day Japan," 273-285.

80 See my article, "The Japanese *Kokutai* [National Community]."

81   See Chie Nakane, *Japanese Society* (Berkeley: University of California Press, 1972).

82   Compare, for example, Edwin O. Reischaurer's article, entitled "Must Korea Be Another Vietnam?" with George F. Will's "Korea, Where 54,246 GIs Died for a Tie," both in Chicago *Sun-Times*, Sunday, June 22, 1975, Section I-A, 3.

83   Gunther, *Inside Asia*, 146.

84   *Ibid.*, 195.

85   Reading George H. Kerr's book *Formosa Betrayed* (New York: Houghton Mifflin, 1965), and Mark Mancall's review of the book entitled "The House that Chiang Unbuilt," *Book Week*, Jan. 23, 1966, 3, will give some insight into this tragic turn of events. Ironically, it was Chiang Kai-shek himself who once said, "no nation can ruin us, unless we first ruin ourselves" as though to prophesy his own destiny.

86   See J.M. Kitagawa, "One of Many Faces of China: Maoism as a Quasi-Religion," *Japanese Journal of Religious Studies*, I, Nos. 2-3 (June-September, 1974), 125-141.

87   See, for example, Roscoe Drummond, "China's Game in Africa," *Chicago Sun-Times*, May 20, 1965, 88.

88   See Ted Gup's article, "The Gang of 1 Billion," Chicago *Sun-Times*, December 30, 1986, 29.
     Certainly recent events have made this last statement abundantly clear; furthermore, I doubt if anyone can truly believe that the authoritarian measures taken following the Tiananmen Massacre in June 1989 will deter peoples' longing for peace and freedom.

89   D.J. Elwood, ed., *Asian Christian Theology: Emerging Themes,* Rev. Ed. (Philadelphia: Westminster, 1980), 44.

90   See R. Tsunoda, *Sources of Japanese Tradition*, section on Uchimura Kanzō, "How I became a Christian," 848-892; see also Irwin Scheiner, *Christian Converts and Social Protest in Meiji Japan* (Berkeley: University of California Press, 1970).

91   See E. Brunner, "A Unique Christian Mission: The Mukyokai ['Non-Church'] Movement in Japan," in W. Leibrecht, ed., *Religion and Culture: Essays in Honor of Paul Tillich* (New York: Harper, 1959), 287-290.

92 See G.B. Bikle, Jr., *The New Jerusalem: Aspects of Utopianism in the Thought of Kagawa Toyohiko* (Tuscon: The University of Arizona Press, 1976).

93 See F.P. Jones, ed., *Documents of the Three-Self Movement* (New York: National Council of the Churches of Christ in the U.S.A., 1963); one of the most up-to-date sources of information about CCPA is found in every issue of *China Update*, edited by Joseph J. Spae, CICM, published in Oud-Heverlee, Belgium.

94 Raul S. Manglapus, "Philippine Culture and Modernization," in Bellah, *Religion and Progress*, 41.

95 See J.W. Heisig, "Facing Religious Pluralism in Asia," in *Inter-Religio*—a newsletter of Christian Organizations for Interreligious Encounters in Eastern Asia—No. 4 (Fall 1983), 34-35.

96 A Catholic approach may be exemplified by *Christianity Meets Buddhism* by H. Dumoulin, S.J. (La Salle: Open Court, 1974); a Protestant view may be seen in M. Doi, "Dialogue between Living Faiths in Japan," *Japanese Religions*, VI, No. 3 (August 1970), 49-73; and *idem, Search for Meaning: Through Inter-Faith Dialogue* (Tokyo: Kyo Bun Kwan, 1976).

97 Quoted in Elwood, *Asian Christian Theology*, 26; emphases added by Elwood.

98 Walter Freytag, *Spiritual Revolution in the East* (London: Butterworth Press, 1940), 18-19.

99 Quoted in Bellah, *Religion and Progress*, xv.

Appendix 1: Some Remarks on Buddhism[1]

Like other world religions, Buddhism of course can be approached—as indeed it has been approached—from a wide variety of perspectives. As an historian of religions with more than casual interests in Buddhism, on this occasion I would like to reflect on the relevance of Buddhism in our time and in the years to come. But first let me make some observations about religion in general.

There was a time—and it was only yesterday—when it was taken for granted that one's affirmation of a religious tradition automatically meant his/her rejection of all other religious options. But it is quite common in our time for non-Jews to read Martin Buber, non-Hindus to read Sarvepalli Radhakrishnan, non-Buddhists to read D.T. Suzuki, and non-Christians to read Paul Tillich, etc. It was also held by many until not so long ago that one had to decide to be either intellectual or pious, because it was assumed to be impossible for one to be both simultaneously. Happily, today increasing numbers of scholars do not hesitate to discuss religious matters publicly, while many devout people are not afraid of scholarly discourses on religions. On the other hand, there are still many oversimplified and erroneous notions about religions that circulate unchecked in many quarters. For example, an amazing number of people say—and evidently they believe—that religion is a private, individual matter which has little relevance to other serious dimensions of life, e.g., social, economic and political activities. Another misleading statement tells us that religion is doomed to die sooner or later in the face of the rising tide of secularism. We are interested to discover that recent events tend to dispel both of these notions, however. Firstly, religion, far from being a harmless individual matter, is deeply involved in important events of the world, e.g.,

conflicts between Catholics and Protestants in Northern Ireland,
between Sinhalese Buddhists and Tamil Hindus in Sri Lanka, between Jews and Muslims in the Middle East, to say nothing about
the religious factors involved in the rise of President Aquino in the
Philippines or the strange phenomenon of Ayatollah Khomeini in
Iran. Also, those who predicted the demise of religion based on
the statistical decline of sabbath attendance in the mainline Jewish
and Christian groups were surprised to discover the steady growth
of new and eclectic religious cults in Africa, Asia, and the Americas, the vitality of the "electronic" churches, the charismatic movements and the now infamous T.V. evangelists in North America,
and the dramatic entry of women into the ranks of religious leadership, despite resistance on the part of some religious leaders.

* * * * *

During World War II I found myself spending over three years
and half in internment camps (euphemistically called "relocation
centers") for Japanese-Americans and their parents in the Inter-
mountain Area in America. You can well imagine that we had no
decent libraries or reading materials, but we read almost every
book or journal we could get hold of. Among all the things I thus
read at random, I still remember one article, even though I don't
recall whether it was in a book or a journal. At any rate, it had
something to do with the kind of post-war world people were en-
visaging, and the author of the article which moved me was talking
about the state of religion. If I remember correctly, the author was
saying that he wanted religions in the post-war era to have at least
three characteristics: "simplicity, sincerity and sympathy." In his
opinion, religions had become too complicated and difficult, over-
laid by far too many doctrines or dogmas, meaningless rituals, and
ecclesiastical forms, customs and obligations. It was important for
religions therefore to regain their original simplicity. Secondly, religions have lost credibility, primarily because they lack sincerity.
Religious leaders teach one thing but practice something else.
There was no correlation between religious rhetorics and actual

religious agendas. The most devastating aspect of religions, in his opinion, was the absence of decent sympathy with men and women, old and young, who struggle with daily problems, disappointments, sorrows and sickness. Certainly, you cannot possibly help or heal all of them, but you can weep and suffer with them or at least comfort them with your sympathetic smiles and words instead of giving only fancy, complicated and impractical theories and generalities.

For some reason, that article spoke to me. I knew only too well what the author of the article was saying. To be sure, in those days my fellow evacuees and I had food and shelter, and we were not expected to engage in forced labor. But we were secluded in a camp surrounded by barbed wire and watchtowers with soldiers and guns. Being a newcomer and an alien, then, I did not expect "royal treatment" in a country at war. But most of the people in our camp were native-born American citizens who were driven out of their homes on the West Coast and incarcerated without any due process of law. And, as someone poignantly observed, "the center was a place where Caucasian people governed and Japanese people were governed. Everything they saw, day in and day out, indicated that racial difference was identical with caste distinction. They were all Americans, but those with white skins were, by virtue of their color, superior to those with colored skin."[2] Indeed, all of us in the camp were compelled to learn by bitter experience that freedom, justice, human dignity, and decency were just as important as food and shelter, if not more.

One of the few inexpensive pleasures allowed to us in the camp was listening to the radio, and I often heard talks by famous individuals of various religious groups. Much to my disappointment, most of the so-called religious messages were nothing but unsolicited war-time propaganda urging men and women to be law-abiding, patriotic and moral citizens and fight for the preservation of democratic values, or else they touted self-righteous sectarianism as the eternal truth. On the other hand, we came in contact with the Quakers and members of other Peace groups, and were greatly touched by their quiet, gentle, selfless attitude toward those who needed assistance, sympathy, kindness and caring. And, from those days in the camp until now I have found it very difficult to trust any religion, however satisfying it may be intellectually, unless it makes people behave more like human beings and exhibits the qualities of "simplicity, sincerity and sympathy."

Being cooped up in an internment camp during the war gave me time and opportunity to think about the intricate relationship between religion and the government. Someone—probably George Bernard Shaw, but I cannot be certain—said that war can so easily transform the religion of peace into an institution of blind, complacent and self-righteous patriotism, or something to that effect, and there is much truth in that observation. I am inclined to believe also that, even without war, religion has often been dominated by the political aims of the state. There are many who assert that only adjusting to political realities can a religion attain power, prestige and practical influence, and they seem to approve government control of religion, citing such examples as King Aśoka (r., c. 274-232 B.C.) who made Buddhism the official religion of his empire in India, and the Emperor Constantine (A.D. 274-337), who made Christianity an official religion of the Roman Empire.

Of course, I have great admiration for both Aśoka and Constantine for having made, respectively, the humble religion of northeastern Indian mendicants and the insignificant religion attributed to a youthful Galilean carpenter into enormously powerful and influential world-wide religions. Even then I cannot help but lament the fact that both Buddhism and Christianity have lost important features of their earlier (or original) qualities and orientations in order to serve as guides to the earthly kingdoms.

I have no intention of boring readers by rehearsing the ambiguous history of early Buddhism, except to say that it is a mistake to regard Buddhism as an offshoot of Brahmanic-Hinduism, as many Hindu scholars and some Buddhist scholars tend to do. Buddhism was an autonomous expression of the religious experience of Buddha and the early Buddhist community, and only after Buddha's demise did Buddhism begin to appropriate idioms and symbols of encroaching Brahmanic-Hinduism to articulate its beliefs, thoughts, and expressions. It should be remembered also that

Buddhism began, as E.J. Thomas stated, "not with a body of doctrine, but with the formation of a [community] bound by certain rules."[3] The Buddhist community came into existence with the firm belief that *Dhamma* (or *Dharma* in Sanskrit, "the liberating law") discovered and proclaimed by the Buddha, could be realized and actualized only in the corporate life of the Buddhist Community (*Saṅgha* in Pali; *Saṃgha* in Sanskrit). Hence the ancient affirmation of the three-fold refuge in the Buddha, Dharma, and Saṃgha. The primary concern of Buddhism was not the existence of human beings in a particular society but the liberation of all beings—"How can they attain Nirvāṇa?"—in the *loka* (the three spheres of existence that comprise the whole universe).

The history of Buddhism took a decisive turn in the third century B.C. with the conversion of King Aśoka, who in the opinion of Charles Eliot was not so much "a pious emperor as an archbishop possessed of exceptional temporal power."[4] Indeed Aśoka, like mother of pearl, appears differently if one looks at him from different angles. Certainly, as he proclaimed in the Bairāt Buddhist Text Edict, he was a pious Buddhist, proud of his "great reverence for and faith in Buddha, the Dharma [and] the Saṃgha."[5] In the eyes of most Buddhists he was truly the Buddhist king par excellence, often identified with the popular image of the universal monarch (*cakravartin*). If you look at him from the side of Hinduism, however, he appears to be every bit a Hindu king, mindful of the traditional Hindu king's duty as a protector of all faiths known in the realm, certainly not only of Buddhism, but of the traditions of the *Brāhmaṇas*, *Śramaṇas*, *Ājīvikas*, Jains, etc., as recorded in Rock Edict 12.[6] His agenda was naturally to govern his empire, and he approached Buddhism from his own kingly perspective. He hammered out a Buddhist-Brahmanic synthetic view of reality on two levels—the "Three Jewels," consisting of the Buddha, Dharma, and the Saṃgha, on the one hand, and a second triad, i.e., the kingship, Dharma (with the accent on justice or law), and the Buddhist inspired state—both triads being grounded in the supreme Law (Dharma) of the deified Buddha. (Parenthetically, Aśoka's concept of Dharma ["justice or law"], authenticated though it was by Buddhism, was in effect a pan-Indian moral principle, and he did not make reference to Nirvāṇa, as many scholars have pointed out.)

According to Aśoka's scheme, the king has not only temporal power but religious authority. Thus, in a manner uncharacteristic of a humble Buddhist, he dared to say: "Whatever the Lord Buddha has said, Reverend Sirs, is of course well said. But it is proper for me to enumerate the texts which express the true Dharma and which make it everlasting."[7] Not only did he thus claim the prerogative to evaluate doctrines, but he also exercised the authority to discipline monks and nuns. He even boasted power to "forgive those who can be forgiven; and, for that they may be induced by me to practice the Dharma; and, that they may attain (the happiness of) this world and of the next world."[8] Under Aśoka, the empire became a gigantic religious state and the headquarters of Buddhist missionaries who were sent to various parts of India and abroad. What Aśoka envisaged was a spiritual conquest (*Dharma-vijaya*)—"Like a conqueror and a ruler who would establish governments in countries politically conquered by him, so Aśoka probably thought of establishing the Sāsana [religion, meaning Buddhism] in countries spiritually conquered . . . by him."[9]

No one can belittle Aśoka's great devotion and contribution to the cause of Buddhism. Nevertheless, one can see great differences between the early Buddhist emphasis on urging people to enter the stream in the hope of attaining *Nirvāṇa* and the Aśokan emphasis on reshaping the world for the spiritual benefit and happiness of men and women. Also, after the time of Aśoka the religious base shifted from the Saṃgha as the "community of faith" to the Buddhist-inspired state, demarcated by its "boundaries" (*sīmā*). Unfortunately, schismatic tendencies which threatened the unity of the Buddhist community became accentuated after Aśoka's time with the result that Buddhism was split into the Hīnayāna (or Theravāda) and Mahāyāna traditions.

It is interesting to note that similar transformations took place in Christianity under the Emperor Constantine. Briefly stated, Christianity arose within the Jewish fold as a charismatic movement.

When the early Christians realized that the end of the world, which had been the eschatological foundation of their faith, might not come soon or that it had already been partially actualized in the Pentecost event, they had to come to terms with the social realities of their time. Initially, they had a realistic understanding of being a religious minority, surrounded by a variety of cultic and religious traditions. For example, the Apostle Paul wrote (in 1 Cor. 8:5-6): "For if there are so-called Gods, whether in Heaven or on the earth—indeed there are many such Gods and many Lords—but to us there is one God, the Father . . . and one Lord. . . ." With Constantine's initiative in making Christianity the religion of the state, a move later amplified by Emperor Theodosius, such a modest understanding of Christianity's place in society was replaced by spiritual arrogance and this-worldly aspiration. Peter Brown writes about the state of Christianity at the time of Augustine (A.D. 354-430)—shortly after the reign of Constantine—that "it reflects the attitude of a group confident of its powers to absorb the world without losing its identity." He goes on to say: "It is a group no longer committed to defend itself against society; but rather poised, ready to fulfil what is considered its historic mission, to dominate, to absorb, to lead a whole Empire. *Ask me, and I shall give the uttermost parts of the earth as Thy possession.*"[10] Undoubtedly Christianity, which had been earlier the community of the faithful in this world but not of this world, gained wealth, power and prestige after the time of Constantine, whereby the *Sacerdotium* rivaled the *Imperium* for worldly influences and authority but at the expense of its earlier orientation as the eschatological religious community.

I am sure there are many other religions which have been "domesticated" so as to be made more palatable as this-worldly "religious" systems eager to serve the needs and the ends of the earthly sovereign nations, or themselves aspiring to become sovereign in all but name, although Buddhism and Christianity are probably the most dramatic, and "successful," examples of this common phenomenon.

Even the most superficial reading of the history of Buddhism makes one aware of the development of three secondary centers of expansion—(1) Ceylon (now Sri Lanka) for the Southern or Theravāda tradition, (2) China for the Northern or Mahāyāna tradition, and (3) Tibet for the Tantric or Esoteric tradition. These three traditions might be called syntheses of religion, culture, society and political order, which constitute discrete, unified organisms. The southern tradition may be characterized as the intricate homology of Theravāda Buddhism with features of Hindu religion, art and culture, chthonic elements in South and Southeast Asia, local societies and political structures. The northern tradition developed a fusion of Mahāyāna Buddhism, features of local religions and cultures (e.g., Confucianism and Taoism in China, Shinto in Japan, etc.) and social and political orders of the localities involved. In a similar vein, the Esoteric tradition blended Tantric Buddhism with certain aspects of the local Bon religion, Tibetan and Mongolian arts and cultures as well as social and political frameworks.

If the above description of Buddhist development—brief and superficial though it is—is reasonably correct, we are confronted by major issues at least on two levels. Firstly, how successfully or genuinely was the Indian Buddhist tradition—itself a composite of syntheses—transmitted to the three secondary centers? On another level, we have to be more aware of how each of the three Buddhist traditions dealt with the inter-cultural and inter-human factors that were so sharply raised by Oswald Spengler. As he pointed out: "Two cultures [involved within each of the Buddhist traditions, for example] may touch between man and man, or the man of one Culture may be confronted by the dead-form-world of another as presented in its communicable relics. In both cases the agent is man himself. The closed-off act of A can be vivified by B only out of his own being, and *eo ipso* it becomes B's, his inward property, his work, and part of himself."[11]

If we should follow Spengler's logic, we have to question whether there was a successful transmission of, say, Mahāyāna Buddhism from China to Japan via Korea—or between Buddhism in India to China. What was transmitted was a certain kind of spiritual tendency, from India to China, or from China to Japan, which became actualized as new modes of religious expressions. Spengler believed that "what matters in all such cases is not the original meaning of the forms, but the forms themselves, as disclosing to the native sensibility and understanding of the observer potential modes of his own creativeness. Connotations are not transferrable. . . ."[12] This is not an idle intellectual issue. In fact it is bound to be raised in our time. For example, we have already a number of Buddhist groups in the West, e.g., Thai and Laotian, the Pure Land, Zen, and Tibetan groups, and a number of new groups still being established. How shall we understand the various "Buddhisms" they represent and how will these groups understand themselves and each other?

Ironically, most people are not aware that Buddhism in the West faces double or triple problems of communication. For example, as dramatically illustrated by the *Sacred Books of the East*, it was Western scholars who initiated the study of non-Western religions, including Buddhism, in the late nineteenth and twentieth centuries using Western critical methods that were eventually adopted by native scholars themselves. In this respect, Buddhist scholars in Japan were exemplary. As early as 1876—less than a decade after the decline of feudalism—Nanjō (also spelled Nanjiō by his preference) Bunyū (d. 1927), a priest of the East Honganji Sect, was dispatched to Oxford to study under Max Müller, editor of the *Sacred Books of the East* among other things. It was Nanjō who published in 1883 *A Catalogue of the Chinese Translations of the Buddhist Tripitaka*. Following his example, a host of able Buddhist scholars studied abroad. Those Japanese Buddhist scholars learned not only Western critical methods for the study of Buddhism and other Eastern religions but also modern Western languages and research languages, such as Sanskrit, Pali, Tibetan and Mongolian, and also Western philosophies. Already in the 1890's, Kiyozawa Manshi or Manji (d. 1903) adopted Hegelianism to articulate his devotion to the grace of Amida. With the publication of *Zen no Kenkyū* ("A Study of Good") by Nishida Kitaro (d. 1945), Nishida and his fellow philosophers and disciples came to be referred to as the "Kyoto

School." As one of the Kyoto philosophers, Takeuchi Yoshinori (1913-) states: "Adopting Western methods, utilizing Western categories and at the same time criticizing both, [these Buddhist philosophers in Kyoto] endeavor to find a new way to express original philosophical insights and often, in view of the results so far achieved, their own life and world views, nurtured in the tradition of Oriental thought."[13] Similar efforts in other Buddhist nations were made, notably by Dharmapāla (d. 1919) of Ceylon, founder of the Maha Bodhi Society, and Abbot T'ai-hsü (d. 1947) of China. All of them were happy to present Buddhism in such a way that it can be understood by Westerners at least superficially, but very few asked the far-reaching question as to whether they were really explicating Buddhism or merely some form of spiritual tendency *à la* Spengler. Unfortunately, their efforts have given the erroneous impression to Western scholars of Buddhism and to Western Buddhists that Western categories and methods are reliable tools to study the meaning of Buddhism.

The pitfall of resorting to the easy way out—by depending primarily on Western language, concepts and methods—was pointed out by D.T. Suzuki already five decades ago. (It is ironic because it was he who almost single-handedly introduced Zen to the West— of course through Western languages. He was also personally very close to Nishida Kitarō and other scholars of the Kyoto School, so much so that he is sometimes included as a member of the Kyoto school itself.[14]) Nevertheless, it was Suzuki, who, after a long career of presenting Buddhism to the West, reflected as follows—he was probably talking about his own reactions when he referred to "Buddhists" in general: "Formerly Buddhists were glad to welcome a [Western] approach to their religion. But nowadays a reaction seems to have taken place among them. Instead of relying on scientific arguments for the rationalization of the Buddhist experience they are at present trying to resort to its own dialectics."[15]

I don't claim that I fathom the depth of Suzuki's thought. But I am inclined to feel that he had at least two related but distinct agendas, that is, (i) presenting the Buddhist form or "spiritual tendency," something like what Spengler had in mind, to the West rather than expecting Westerners to understand Buddhism as such, and (ii) reconstructing and reformulating Buddhism itself by retrieving the Buddhist experience of the early community and tracing the historical expansion of Buddhism, quite apart from the consideration as to how much of this effort could be understood by Westerners, or even by contemporary Asian Buddhists themselves, for that matter.

Following his first agenda, Suzuki tried to present the whole gamut of Buddhist literature in English for the benefit of Westerners. In so doing, as Heinrich Dumoulin astutely observes, Suzuki interpreted and "adapted" it to Western ways of thinking, in a way reminiscent of William James, judging from Suzuki's earlier writings· "But this influence was not a merely superficial borrowing of terms. Suzuki felt a certain affinity with [James], who, like himself, esteemed experience above all else and displayed a genuine appreciation of religion."[16]

In his later writings Suzuki exhibited his predilection for philosophical metaphysical thinking, not necessarily bound always by a historical framework. In fact, his tendency to psychologize and his daring habit of uprooting Zen from its native Buddhist soil misled many of his Western disciples, "who heard their revered master say over and over again that Zen was neither a philosophy nor a religion [in the Western sense], [and] proceeded to interpret Zen in their own terms, which were usually alien to traditional Buddhism."[17] Probably Suzuki himself must have felt that the Zen-inspired "spiritual tendency," could be or should be authenticated by the Western spiritual tradition, without cumbersome Buddhist trappings.[18]

The confusing fact about Suzuki was that he followed the two agendas almost simultaneously, so that it was difficult for others to tell which was which at times. Evidently, he was very clear in his own mind when he pursued the second agenda, i.e., reconstructing and reformulating Buddhism itself, as seen in his famous articles "Buddhist Symbolism"[19] (in which he rejected the notion of symbolism for Buddhism) and "An Interpretation of Zen-Experience"[20]—as well as in his numerous articles and books. I am not upholding Suzuki's approach as the paradigmatic solution for the intricate problem of models, paradigms, and communication. But I am impressed by his perception of the nature of the problems involved in the transmission of Buddhism from one cultural context to another (in this case to the West).

It is far from my intention to conclude my reflection with a sense of hopelessness. But I cannot help but feel, following D.T. Suzuki, that we should not underestimate the difficulties of the issues involved in the transmission of Buddhism in our time.

*   *   *   *   *

I would like to add one more item to my unsystematic reflections and remarks on Buddhism, namely the broad issue of models, paradigms, and communication. At this writing, I see on the TV screen the tragic melodramas of the Iran-Contra hearings and the public controversies among popular evangelists, and I am struck by the existence of wide disagreements and discrepancies on the part of people who are supposed to know better, e.g., government officials, military officers, diplomats, lawyers and clerics, about such fundamental notions as justice, patriotism, rights, duty, morality, etc. The roots of this confusion no doubt derive from the Western world's unique convention of demarcating human experience into such domains as religion, philosophy, morality, aesthetics, psychology, politics, etc. We are slowly—and only too slowly—beginning to rectify such a one-sided view. This, however, is not a peculiarly Western problem. The history of Buddhism certainly testifies to the existence of this kind of problem.

Notes

1   The piece was originally written for the inauguration of the Japanese journal, *Bukkyō* ("Buddhism"), Vol. 1, no. 1 (October 1987) (Kyoto: Hozo-kan). I would like to thank the publisher for permission to reprint this article here.

2   Richard Drinnon, *Keeper of Concentration Camps* (Berkeley: University of California Press, 1987), 45.

3   E.J. Thomas, *The History of Buddhist Thought* (New York: Barnes and Noble, 1951), 14.

4   Sir Charles Eliot, *Hinduism and Buddhism* (3 vols.; New York: Barnes and Noble, 1954), I, 265.

5   Amulyachandra Sen, *Aśoka's Edicts* (Calcutta: The Indian Publicity Society, 1956), 30 and 134-135.

6   *Ibid.*, 94.

7   This translation is taken from N.A. Nikam and Richard McKeon, *The Edicts of Aśoka* (Chicago: The University of Chicago Press, 1959), 66.

8   Sen, *Edicts*, 116.

9   Walpola Rahula, *History of Buddhism in Ceylon* (Colombo: Gunasena, 1956), 54-55.

10 Peter Brown, *Augustine of Hippo: A Biography* (Berkeley: University of California Press, 1969), 214.

11 Oswald Spengler, *The Decline of the West* (2 vols.; New York: A.A. Knopf, 1932), II, 57.

12 *Ibid.*

13 Y. Takeuchi, "Modern Japanese Philosophy," *Encyclopaedia Britannica*, 1968 edition, XII, 958J.

14 See Frederick Franck, ed., *The Buddha Eye: An Anthology of the Kyoto School* (New York: Crossroad, 1982).

15 Quoted in A.E. Haydon, ed., *Modern Trends in World-Religions* (Chicago: University of Chicago Press, 1934), 38.

16 H. Dumoulin, *Zen Enlightenment: Origins and Meaning* (New York: Weatherhill, 1979), 5.

17 *Ibid.*, 6-7.

18 Read D.T. Suzuki, *Living by Zen* (New York: Rider, 1950) with this in mind.

19 In L. Bryson *et al.*, eds., *Symbols and Values: An Initial Study* (New York: Conference on Science, Philosophy, and Religion in Relation to the Democratic Way of Life, Inc., 1954), 149-154.

20 See D.T. Suzuki, "An Interpretation of Zen-Experience," in C.A. Moore, ed., *Philosophy—East and West* (Princeton: Princeton University Press, 1946), 109-129.

Appendix 2: Religious Visions of the End of the World[1]

In December, 1982, a tragic event took place in the small community of Murphysboro, Tennessee, U.S.A. A police officer was held hostage for thirty hours by members of a religious cult and was finally beaten to death. This particular cult group apparently believes that the end of the world is imminent and that the Bible identifies the police as the anti-Christs and representatives of the devil prophesied by the Johannine Apocalypse.[2] When my students in Chicago heard about the incident, several of them shrugged their shoulders and dismissed it as one of many such bizarre cult-related happenings. I agreed with them that the fatal beating of a police officer by a presumably religious group is indeed bizarre; but I pointed out that religious visions of the end of the world, however they are understood, have been a persistent and important motif in various religions, both past and present, both in the West and in the East. In this paper, I will discuss how certain religious traditions have viewed the end of the world and how different perceptions of the end of the world have in turn shaped the religious and cultural outlooks of various peoples.

My reflections on this vast problem are based on a simple premise: every religion, every culture, and every civilization has a characteristic outlook toward the future and a characteristic way of recollecting the past; and these together influence the particular understanding of the meaning of present existence. St. Augustine expressed this premise in his statement on time: "There are three *times*: [first] a present of things past, [second] a present of things present, and [third] a present of things future." According to him, the "present of things past" is associated with memory, the "present of things present" with sight, and the "present of things future" with

expectation.[3] These three foci—the expectation of the future, the
recollection of the past, and the understanding of the present—are
intricately woven into a kind of "mental prism" which extracts significant items from a mass of data and relates historical realities to
fancies or fantasy and the imagination. Embedded in this prism are
also the elements of forgetfulness and optical illusion.

The persistent power of the past dimension of the mental prism,
that dimension which recollects past experiences, is forcefully exemplified in our time by the Middle East conflicts[4] or the conflicts
on the subcontinent of India. Equally powerful is the mental
prism's angle of vision for the future, which is undeniably and integrally related to its angle of vision of the past. We are acutely
aware that the future and the present are merely movable dots on
the horizontal line of the continuum of time, as we read in the
haunting words of Macbeth:

> To-morrow, and to-morrow, and to-morrow
> Creeps in this petty pace from day to day,
> To the last syllable of recorded time. . . . [5]

In short, our daily existence assumes the existence of the future;
and, in spite of the scriptural admonition not to be anxious about
tomorrow, "for tomorrow will be anxious for itself" (Matt. 6:34), we
feel that we must be concerned and prepared for the future. There
are, certainly, psychological differences between optimists and pes-
simists, who clearly approach the future differently (despite a new
definition that a pessimist is an optimist with experience). More
significant, however, is the fact that one's perception of the future—whether that future be beneficial or detrimental—has a decisive impact on one's attitude toward the present; and, more often
than not, our perception of the future is heavily influenced by our
religious and cultural outlook.

Take, for example, the notion of progress, a word derived from
the term *gressus*, "step," and connoting the act of stepping forward
to a situation more desirable than the current. In our consideration we must first recognize the difference, as pointed out by Paul
Tillich, between the "concept" of progress, which is an abstraction,

and the "idea" of progress, which is an interpretation of an historical situation, with or without verifiable basis, in terms of the
"concept" of progress. The "idea" of progress thus involves our
mental decision or affirmation; and it becomes a symbol as well as a
way of life, a "doctrine" about the law of history, or even an unconscious "dogma" of progressivism.[6]

The notion that the future promises to be better than the present, leading to the culmination of all values at the end of the
world, clearly is not based on empirical observation, but on speculation and affirmation. Such speculation and affirmation are often
associated with a religious vision of the coming, at the end, of the
cosmic ruler, the universal king or the world savior. In contrast to
this positive form of progressivism, we find as well negative forms,
which view the future in terms of the successive erosion of values,
although they are still often associated with the belief in the coming of a supra-mundane figure who redresses all evils at the end of
the world. Regardless of the positive or negative focus on progressivism, our perceptions of the end of the world, and of the character of the divine figure who appears at the end, as mentioned earlier, influence our attitude toward the present. In the history of religions, we have two prominent figures of cosmic saviors or rulers
who have inspired a series of messianic ideologies, and who have
thus influenced the future outlook of peoples in many parts of the
world. The first is Saošyant of Iranian Zoroastrianism; the second
is the Cakravartin of India.

Saošyant

According to the ancient Iranian religion, Zoroastrianism, history comprises a cosmic conflict between the just god, Ahura Maz-
dah, and the forces of evil. Human beings are destined to choose
sides and to participate in the conflict. Zoroastrianism originally
articulated the notion of the end of the world, the *eschaton*, and
the doctrine of the end, or eschatology: at the end of the cosmic
cycle of 12,000 years, the savior and judge, Saošyant, born miracu-
lously of a maiden and the seed of Zoroaster, will appear and reha-

bilitate creation, casting the Devil into hell and purging the human race from the stain of sin. The whole human race will then enter into paradise, there to enjoy eternal bliss and happiness.

"The significance of Zoroastrianism," writes R.C. Zaehner, "lies not in the number of those who profess it, but rather in the influence it has exercised on other religions [for example, all Gnostic religions—Hermetism, Gnosticism, Manicheism] and particularly on Christianity, through the medium of the Jewish exiles in Babylon, who seem to have been thoroughly impregnated with Zoroastrian ideas." He states further that "Christianity claims to be the heir of the prophets of Israel. If there is any truth in this claim, it is not less heir to the Prophet of ancient Iran, little though most Christians are aware of this fact."[7]

Zoroastrianism exerted an especially strong influence on Jewish eschatology, including the beliefs in the Messianic era of national restoration, the coming of the new *aeon* of God's kingdom, and the celestial hereafter for the deceased; it influenced as well the Jewish comprehension of sacred history, which understands God, who had elected the nation of Israel, as one day fulfilling his promise by establishing his rule on earth. Christianity, which was born as a messianic movement within Judaism, inherited as a matter of course the Iranian-inspired Jewish eschatological perspective; but when early Christians recognized that the anticipated return of Christ (*parousia*, "arrival" or "presence") would not be realized as soon as they had expected—or that it had perhaps already been partially realized at the Pentecost—they were forced to come to terms with the social realities of the current situation. This example graphically illustrates, I think, how a change in the conception of the future causes changes in attitudes toward the present.

The Cakravartin

Indian religious lore gives us an ancient mythical ideal of a just and virtuous world monarch, the Cakravartin ("owner of the wheel [*cakra*]"), a divinely ordained "superman" (*mahāpuruṣa*) who, due to his moral supremacy and moral power, has a special place in the cosmic scheme as the final unifier of the whole earthly realm. Heinrich Zimmer has traced the conception of the Cakravartin "not only to the earliest Vedic, but also the pre-Vedic, pre-Aryan traditions of India, being reflected in various Buddhist and Jain writings, as well as in the Hindu *purāṇas.*"[8] The significance of the Cakravartin lies in the fact that his figure came to be accepted as the monarchical ideal in the later Vedic imperial ideology; in addition, it also provided a paradigm for Buddhist speculations on the person and mission of the Buddha.

Despite numerous legends about the founder of Buddhism, we actually know very little about the Buddha's life: we are not even certain which century he was born in—the sixth or the fifth century B.C. The canonical accounts of his life, written centuries after his death, portray the Buddha as a royal prince, accustomed in his youth to the splendor and luxury of the palace. Most likely, however, he belonged to a minor fighting aristocracy, wealthy according to the standards of the time. His spiritual quest motivated him to leave home to lead the life of a mendicant. We are told that, as he concentrated in deep meditation under a bodhi tree, he saw in a trance a vision of his previous existences. He also gained piercing insight into the meaning of existence and attained the path of emancipation from the transitoriness of the finite world. After his enlightenment experience, he preached the Good Law for over forty years. His mission was to establish a religions community of monastics and laity, the *Saṃgha*, which was not circumscribed by national, racial, or cultural boundaries.

In the course of time, the career of this humble mendicant came to be seen as a spiritual counterpart of the career of the universal monarch, the Cakravartin. Popular Buddhist piety held that the Buddha and the Cakravartin shared the same universal principle and that both had identical marks at birth—the thirty-two great marks. Buddhists believed further that when the Buddha was born, he had the choice to aspire to either the path of the universal ruler (Cakravartin) or the path of the world savior. They appropriated such symbols of the Cakravartin as the sacred wheel (*cakra*), the divine white elephant, the white horse, and the magic jewel (*cintāmaṇi*) for use on their altars and in their relic mounds (*stūpas*), as symbols of the spiritual kingship of the Buddha.[9] They offered rhapsodic praises to the memory of him who is said to have given up an earthly kingdom to establish a spiritual kingdom:

> Unto this came I . . .
> for I will not have that crown
> which may be mine; I lay aside those realms
> which wait the gleaming of my naked swords:
> My chariot shall not roll with bloody wheels
> from victory to victory, till earth
> wears the red record of my name. I choose
> to tread its paths with patient, stainless feet,
> making its dust my bed, its loneliest wastes
> my dwelling, and its meanest things my mates. . . .[10]

In the third century B.C., Buddhism, which had begun as an insignificant religion of mendicants and pious lay people in northeast India, was promoted by King Aśoka as the religion of his vast empire. Although Aśoka never claimed to be the Cakravartin, later Buddhists—especially Buddhist rulers in south and southeast Asia and China—came to regard him as a model of the Buddhist monarch, preshadowing the Buddhist image of the universal monarch (Cakravartin) yet to come.

The Cakravartin, Maitreya, and Amitābha

The Buddhist speculation about the person of the Buddha was not confined to identification with the Cakravartin. Since Buddhist tradition accepted the notion that the Buddha, seated under the bodhi tree, saw a vision of his previous existences, it was not difficult for Buddhists to speculate on the existence of previous Buddhas, or of the three bodies of the Buddha, or of multiple Buddhas, each residing in one of numerous Buddha-fields (*buddha-kṣetra*) which together constitute the cosmos. Furthermore, the stream of foreign religions and art forms that flowed into India from Bactria and Iran, shortly before and after the beginning of the common era, greatly influenced the piety, imagination, and artistic sensitivities of both Hindus and Buddhists. Two examples of prominent Buddhist savior figures who emerged from this fascinating religious and cultural milieu, and who made a decisive impact on Buddhist outlooks on the future, deserve mention here. The first is Maitreya, the future Buddha; the second is Amitābha, the Buddha of the glamorous Western paradise.

Maitreya

The close association of the Buddha with the Cakravartin, the ruler who will unify the whole cosmos at the end of the world, forwarded the belief in Maitreya, the future Buddha whose coming would signify both the fulfillment of the Buddha's Law or Teaching, and the establishment of universal peace and concord. Many scholars believe that Saošyant, the Iranian cosmic savior mentioned earlier, inspired the Buddhist notion of Maitreya. In the opinion of A.L. Basham, "under the invading rulers of Northwest India, Zoroastrianism and Buddhism came in contact, and it was probably through this that the idea of the future Buddha became part of orthodox [Buddhist] belief. . . . [And by the] beginning of the Christian era, the cult of the future Buddha, Maitreya, was widespread among all Buddhists."[11] The Southern tradition of Buddhism—the Small Vehicle (Hīnayāna) or the Tradition of the Elders (Theravāda), followed in Sri Lanka (Ceylon) and Southeast Asian countries—recognizes only the Buddha and Maitreya as Bodhisattvas, or "future Buddhas." According to legend, Maitreya (Metteyya in Pali), like the Buddha, had had many lives before being born as a prince. He, too, forsook his comfortable palace life and he attained Buddhahood under a dragon-flower tree. He now lives as the Lord of the *Tuṣita* heaven until the Buddha's teaching erodes. At that moment he will descend to the world and will hold three assemblies under a dragon-flower tree. Buddhists believe that, at his coming, Buddha's Law, peace, and justice will be restored, and all faithful followers of his path will be able to attain sainthood, or *arhat*ship.

Ironically, in the Southern tradition, the figures of Maitreya, the future Buddha, and the Cakravartin, the universal monarch who will appear at the end of the world, came to be seen as one and the same, and each was adopted by Buddhist kings as a way of legitimizing earthly royal reign. Moreover, many Buddhist kings aspired not only to ascend to Maitreya's heaven, but also to "become" Maitreya in future eras, and gigantic statues of Maitreya were erected throughout their kingdoms. Still and all, the Maitreyan ideal, conceived as a corrective to the ills of the empirical social and political order, never developed. Only in modern times has this idea been infused with a revolutionary impulse, as exemplified by various anti-colonial movements. After Burma's independence, U Nu, who was looked upon by many people as a Buddha in the coming, attempted to establish in Burma an earthly Nirvāṇa, which was to become the dwelling place of the future Buddha, Maitreya, and of saintly hermits. Other attempts to actualize the Maitreyan paradise have been made in our time, and although they have failed, the fact that they have been inspired by the Maitreyan ideal is most significant. For those Buddhists, in particular, who now live in Cambodia, Laos, and Vietnam under regimes hostile to Buddhism, the anticipation of the "descent" of Maitreya may become an important basis for their outlook for the future.

Maitreya and Amitābha

In the Northern tradition—the Great Vehicle or Mahāyāna, that had spread to Central Asia, China, Korea, and Japan—Maitreya was rivalled by the savior figure of Amitābha (the Buddha of Infinite Light), known also as Amitāyus (the Buddha of Infinite Life), a Buddha not recognized by the Southern (Pali) Canon. Amitābha, too, emerged from the cross-cultural and cross-religious milieu that characterized the beginning of the common era, when the connection of divinity and light, or of divinity and the sun, became fashionable through the popularity of deities associated with light, such as Mithra, Helios, and Apollo in Central Asia and Northwestern India. Amitābha Buddha is the Lord of the Western Paradise—Sukhāvatī, the blissful Pure Land—the final home of the sun and all departed spirits.

In China, as in the Southeast Asian countries, the image born of the merging of Maitreya and the universal monarch, the Cakravartin, was appropriated and distorted by rulers eager to enhance their kingship by means of Buddhist symbols. Chinese popular piety developed two types of Maitreya cult, one stressing the motif of "ascent," and another the motif of "descent." Those who followed the "ascent" motif seriously aspired to be reborn in Maitreya's heaven at their death, while those who espoused the "descent" motif, believing that Maitreya might come very soon, hoped to prolong life until then, or to be reborn on earth after Maitreya's arrival, so that they could hear his preaching. The "ascent" motif was gradually eclipsed by the growing popularity of Amitābha, who was believed to have vowed to bring all sentient beings to his blissful Pure Land. Devotees of Amitābha were greatly influenced by the legendary theory of negative progressivism; they firmly believed that the era of the Buddha's teaching was destined to be followed successively by the eras of counterfeit teaching and of the decline and decay of the Buddha's Law, and that the dreaded "last period" was coming soon—if, indeed, it had not arrived already. This sense of urgency, concerning the impending cosmic catastrophe, lent great intensity to their devotion to Amitābha.

Although the "ascent" motif of the Maitreya cult was superseded by worship of Amitābha, the motif of Maitreya's "descent" thoroughly penetrated the consciousness of the Chinese populace, especially that of members of the sectarian movements which arose outside of orthodox Buddhism. For those oppressed by, and dissatisfied with, social, political, and economic injustices, the Maitreyan eschatological vision was compelling, as attested by the series of rebel and revolutionary movements which have marked Chinese history from the seventh to the nineteenth centuries.

In Korea and Japan as well, the Maitreya cult attracted many devotees; but the movement soon lost its eschatological and prophetic character due to the rapid assimilation of Buddhism into the cultural and national fabric of both countries. In the twelfth and thirteenth centuries, Japan was beset by natural calamities, social unrest, and political instability, all accepted as confirmation of the arrival of the dreaded era of the decay of Buddhism. The cult of Amitābha, at this time, stimulated the growth of intense pietistic movements, for example, the Pure Land School, the True Pure Land School, and the Nichiren School. As the sense of impending doom lessened, however, Amitābha followers in Japan, not unlike the early Christians, lost their eschatological fervor and adjusted themselves to the realities of a mundane society. During the last century, when the foundations of a still feudal society were shaken by both external and internal agents, the "descent" motif of Maitreya significantly inspired movements to rectify the social order, movements exemplified by an emergent series of messianic cults.

The Impact of the Modern West on Asia

The disintegration of the cultures of Asia during the past four or five centuries is beyond the scope of this discussion; we can only state that the slow process of internal stagnation in Asia was accelerated by the advance of the West during the eighteenth and nineteenth centuries. Since the Renaissance, Western civilization has acquired all the earmarks of a pseudo-religion of secularized salvation, and Westerners have become convinced that the West alone was the inventor and transmitter of true civilization, to be propagated for the edification of the "backward" peoples of the non-Western world. The combined forces of Western civilization, Christian missionary enterprise, and colonial expansion effected social, political, economic, cultural, and religious changes in much of Asia and Africa by the end of the nineteenth century. Democracy was the theology of Western civilization, and science its holy writ. The new gospel of secular salvation—liberty, equality and fraternity, and modernity—attracted both the intelligentsia and the iconoclastic youths in the non-Western world, who had "inhaled" the dogma of the modern West, the idea of "progress here and now," and had discarded the traditional ideas of otherworldly rewards, in the life to come in the heaven of either Maitreya or Amitābha.

When viewed from the perspective of the non-Western world, the significance of Wilson and Lenin, two secular saviors who emerged on the world scene after World War I, is readily apprehended. Each offered a universal program of peace and plenty; but Lenin's Russian Revolution did not achieve a world-wide utopia for the oppressed, and Wilson's League of Nations did not eradicate Western colonial imperialism. Deeply disappointed in both the Russian and the Western options, non-Western peoples were thus driven to find their own alternatives, alternatives which included political independence and the restoration of their neglected cultural and religious traditions. The emergence of independent nations in Asia after World War II—the Philippines (1946); India and Pakistan (1947); Ceylon (Sri Lanka), Burma, South and North Korea (1948); Indonesia and the Peoples Republic of China (1949); Vietnam (1954); Cambodia (1955); Laos (1956); the Federation of Malaya (1957); to say nothing of the new nations in Africa—not only signified the end of modern Western colonialism, but also represented the beginning of a process by which peoples of the non-Western world could redefine their concepts of dignity, value, and freedom.

It is ironic that these new nations in Asia and Africa have attained political independence after the end of the era of the nation-state. Leaders of these nations increasingly understand that the real problems which confront them are not soluble within the confines of the egocentric sovereign nation, or within quarrelsome regional communities of nations. They cannot even approach the still rich and powerful Western nations to solve these problems, as Walter Lippman warned us two decades ago, the great powers can no longer govern the affairs of the world. Trapped in this dilemma, we might indulge in romantic nostalgia for a lost paradise, and attempt to solve today's problems with yesterday's answers; or we might cling to both new and old forms of millenarian options. Our task, however, is to discern the real nature of our uncertain future, for it is as true today as it was yesterday that our perception of the future determines our attitude toward the present.

Some fifteen years ago, Claude Lévi-Strauss, the noted French anthropologist, stated in his comments on the unrest of the younger generation, the acceleration of population growth, the advancement of militarization, and the increased exploitation of energy that "man, who since the Renaissance has been brought up to adore himself," must learn a new meaning of modesty. "He would do well to learn that if one thinks only man is respectable among living beings . . . he can no longer be protected. One must first consider that it is as a living being that [the human being] is worthy of respect. . . ."[12] Such a shift in our thinking, in Lévi-Strauss' view, will take "a spiritual revolution" of great magnitude. While such a realization alone may not solve our problems, it might at least give us the courage to live responsibly in our time, without either indulging in wishful thinking or falling into despair. If not, our future is indeed bleak.

Notes

1 This essay was originally contributed to *GILGUL: Essays on Transformation, Revolution and Permanence in the History of Religions* — dedicated to R.J. Zwi Werblowsky, and edited by S. Shaked, D. Shulman and G.G. Stroumsa (Leiden: E.J. Brill, 1987). I would like to thank the publisher for permission to reprint the article here.

2 *Chicago Sun-Times*, January 16, 1983.

3 Augustine, "The Confessions," trans. E.B. Pusey, *Great Books of the Western World* (36 vols.; Chicago: Encyclopedia Britannica, Inc., 1952), XVIII, 52.

4 Cf. I.F. Stone, "Holy War" (review of "Le Conflit israelo-arabe") in *New York Times Review of Books* (August 3, 1967), 6.

5 William Shakespeare, *Macbeth*, V.5.

6 Paul Tillich, *The Future of Religions*, ed. J.C. Brauer (New York: Harper and Row, 1966), 64ff.

7 R.C. Zaehner, "Zoroastrianism," in R.C. Zaehner, ed., *The Concise Encyclopedia of Living Faiths* (New York: Hawthorn Books, 1959), 209.

8 Heinrich Zimmer, *Philosophies of India*, ed. Joseph Campbell (New York: Pantheon Books, 1951), 129.

9 *Ibid.*, 130-31.

10 Sir Edwin Arnold, *The Light of Asia and the Indian Song of Praise* (Bombay: Jaico Publishing House, 1949), Bk. 4, 63.

11 A.L. Basham, *The Wonder That Was India* (New York: Grove Press, 1954), 274.

12 Cited in John L. Hess, "French Anthropologist, at onset of 70's, deplores the 20th century," *New York Times*, December 31, 1969.

Works Consulted

A. Books and Articles within Books

Abegg, Lily. *The Mind of East Asia*. London: Thames & Hudson, 1952.

Adams, Charles J. "Islam in Pakistan," in Kitagawa, J.M., ed., *Modern Trends in World Religions*. La Salle: Open Court, 1959.

Anshen, R.N., ed. *Moral Principles of Action*. New York: Harper, 1952.

Bain, C.A. *The Far East*. Ames: Littlefield, Adams & Co., 1952.

Ball, W. MacMahon. *Nationalism and Communism in East Asia*. Melbourne: University Press, 1952.

Basham, A.L. *The Wonder That Was India*. New York: Grove Press, 1954.

Bellah, R.N., ed. *Religion and Progress in Modern Asia*. New York: The Free Press, 1965.

Benz, Ernst. *Buddhism or Communism: Which Holds the Future of Asia?* New York: Doubleday, 1965.

Bikle, G.B. Jr. *The New Jerusalem: Aspects of Utopianism in the Thought of Kagawa Toyohiko*. Tucson: The University of Arizona Press, 1976.

Bishop, C.W. "The Beginning of Civilization in Eastern Asia," in *The Beginnings of Civilization in the Orient*, Supplement to the *Journal of the American Oriental Society*, No. 4, December 1939.

Bodde, Derk. *Essays on Chinese Civilization*. Princeton: Princeton University Press, 1981.

The Book of Common Prayer. New York: The Church Hymnal Corporation, 1977.

Bowles, C. *Ambassador's Report*. New York: Harper, 1954.

Brown, Peter. *Augustine of Hippo*. Berkeley: University of California Press, 1967.

Brunner, E. "A Unique Christian Mission: The Mukyokai ['Non-Church'] Movement in Japan," in Leibrecht, W., ed., *Religion and Culture: Essays in Honor of Paul Tillich*. New York: Harper, 1959.

Cameron, Nigel. *Barbarians and Mandarins*. New York: Walker/Weatherhill, 1970.

Cartlidge, D.R. & D.L. Dungan. *Documents for the Study of the Gospels*. Philadelphia: Fortress Press, 1980.

Chalmers, Lord (Robert), ed. and tr. *Buddha's Teachings, being the Sutta-nipāta, or, Discourse-Collection*. Harvard Oriental Series, vol. 37; Cambridge: Harvard University Press, 1932.

Chan, Chen-chi. *The Practice of Zen*. New York: Harper, 1959.

Chan, Wing-tsit, I.R. al Fārūqī, J.M. Kitagawa & P.T. Raju. *The Great Asian Religions: An Anthology*. New York: Macmillan, 1969.

Chan, Wing-tsit. "The Concept of Man in Chinese Philosophy," in Radhakrishnan, S. & P.T. Raju, eds., *The Concept of Man*. London: G. Allen & Unwin, 1960.

Charles, G.P. "Let God Speak," in *Burmese Christian Council Annual*. Rangoon, 1953.

Ch'en, Kenneth K.S. *The Chinese Transformation of Buddhism*. Princeton: Princeton University Press, 1973.

Christy, A.E., ed. *The Asian Legacy and American Life*. New York: John Day, 1942.

Cnattingius, H. *Bishops and Societies*. London: S.P.C.K., 1952.

The Commission of Appraisal: *Re-Thinking Missions*. New York: Harper, 1932.

Coomaraswamy, A.K. *Hinduism and Buddhism*. New York: Philosophical Library, 1943.

Daniel, N. *Islam and the West — The Making of an Image*. Edinburgh: The University Press, 1960.

Dawson, Christopher. *Enquiries into Religion and Culture*. London: Sheed & Ward, 1933.

Dean, Vera M. *The Nature of the Non-Western World*. New York: The New American Library: A Mentor Book, 1957.

Denny, F.M. & R.L. Taylor, eds. *The Holy Book in Comparative Perspective*. Columbia: University of South Carolina Press, 1985.

Devanandan, Paul & M.M. Thomas, eds. *Communism and Social Revolution in India*. Calcutta: Y.M.C.A., 1953.

Djait, H. *Europe and Islam.* Berkeley: University of California Press, 1985.

Doi, M. *Search for Meaning: Through Inter-Faith Dialogue.* Tokyo: Kyo Bun Kwan, 1976.

Dumoulin, H., S.J. *Christianity Meets Buddhism.* La Salle: Open Court, 1974.

Dye, J.W. & W.H. Forthman. *Religions of the World: Selected Readings.* New York: Appleton Century Crofts, 1957.

Earle, Wm. *Public Sorrows and Private Pleasures.* Bloomington: Indiana University Press, 1976.

Ebrey, Patricia E., ed. *Chinese Civilization and Society: A Sourcebook.* New York: Macmillan, 1981.

Eliade, Mircea. *Yoga: Immortality and Freedom.* New York: Pantheon Books, *Bollingen Series*, LVI, 1958.

_____. *Myths, Dreams and Mysteries.* New York: Harper, 1960.

_____. *No Souvenirs: Journal, 1957-1969.* New York: Harper, 1977.

_____. *Ordeal by Labyrinth: Conversations with Claude-Henri Rocquet.* Chicago: The University of Chicago Press, 1982.

Eliade, Mircea, ed. *The Encyclopedia of Religion.* New York: Macmillan, 1987-1988.

Elwood, D.J., ed. *Asian Christian Theology: Emerging Themes,* rev. ed. Philadelphia: Westminster, 1980.

"Enlightenment." *The New Encyclopaedia Britannica: Micropaedia*, 15th ed., vol. IV, 1985.

"European Overseas Exploration and Empires." *The New Encyclopaedia Britannica: Macropaedia*, 15th ed., vol. XVIII, 1985.

Fairbank, J.K., ed. *The Missionary Enterprise in China and America*. Cambridge: Harvard University Press, 1974.

Fehl, Noah E. *History and Society*. Hong Kong: Chung Chi College, 1964.

Finegan, J. *The Archeology of World Religions*. Princeton: Princeton University Press, 1952.

Freytag, Walter. *Spiritual Revolution in the East*. London: Lutterworth Press, 1940.

Garbe, Richard. *India and Christendom: The Historical Connections Between Their Religions*. La Salle: The Open Court, 1959.

Gibb, H.A.R. *Mohammedanism: A Historical Survey*. London: Oxford University Press, 1953.

_____. "Near Eastern Perspective: The Present and the Future," in Young, T.C., ed., *Near Eastern Culture and Society*. Princeton: Princeton University Press, 1951.

Girling, J.L.S. *Thailand: Society and Politics*. Ithaca: Cornell University Press, 1981.

Grodzins, Morton. *Americans Betrayed: Politics and the Japanese Evacuation*. Chicago: The University of Chicago Press, 1949.

Grousett, René. *Chinese Art and Culture*. New York: Grove Press, 1959.

_____. *The Rise and Splendour of Chinese Empire*. Berkeley: University of California Press, 1952.

Grunebaum, G.E. von. *Medieval Islam*. Chicago: The University of Chicago Press, 1946.

Grunebaum, G.E. von, ed. *Unity and Variety in Muslim Civilization*. Chicago: The University of Chicago Press, 1955.

Gunther, John. *Inside Asia*. New York: Harper, 1939.

Haas, Wm. S. *The Destiny of the Mind: East and West*. London: Faber & Faber, 1956.

Hakim, K.A. "One God, One Word, One Humanity," in Anshen, *Moral Principles of Action*. New York: Harper, 1952.

Hardy, P. "Islam in South Asia," in Eliade, *The Encyclopaedia of Religion*, vol. VII. New York: Macmillan, 1987-1988.

Heimann, Betty. *Indian and Western Philosophy: A Study of Contrasts*. London: G. Allen & Unwin, 1937.

Henderson, John B. *The Development and Decline of Chinese Cosmology*. New York: Columbia University Press, 1984.

Hinson, E.G. "Irenaeus," in Eliade, *The Encyclopaedia of Religion*, vol. VII. New York: Macmillan, 1987-1988.

Hitti, P.K. *The Arabs — A Short History*. Princeton: Princeton University Press, 1949.

Hocking, W.E. *Living Religions and A World Faith*. New York: Macmillan, 1940.

Hodgson, Marshall G.S. *The Venture of Islam*, 3 vols. Chicago: The University of Chicago Press, 1974.

Hoffman, R. "Propaganda, Sacred Congregation of," in Neill, S. et. al. (eds.), *Concise Dictionary of the Christian Mission*. Nashville: Abingdon Press, 1971.

Hopkins, T. *The Hindu Religious Tradition*. Encino: Dickenson, 1971.

Hutchins, R.M. *The Great Conversation (Great Books of the Western World*, I). Chicago: E.B. 1951.

Hutchinson, J.A. *Paths of Faith*. New York: McGraw Hill, 1969.

Isaacs, Harold. *Scratches on the Mind*. New York: John Day, 1958.

Jansen, Marius. *Japan and Its World*. Princeton: Princeton University Press, 1980.

Jay, Martin. *Marxism and Totality*. Berkeley: University of California Press, 1974.

Jennings, J.C. *The Vedantic Buddhism of Buddha*. London: Oxford University Press, 1948.

Johns, A.H. "Islam in Southeast Asia," in Eliade, *The Encyclopaedia of Religion*, vol. VII. New York: Macmillan, 1987-1988.

Jones, E.P., ed. *Documents of the Three-Self Movement*. New York: National Council of the Churches of Christ in the U.S.A., 1963.

King, W.L. *A Thousand Lives Away: Buddhism in Contemporary Burma*. Cambridge: Harvard University Press, 1964.

King, Winston L. "Religion," in Eliade, *The Encyclopaedia of Religion*, vol. XII. New York: Macmillan, 1987-1988.

Kitagawa, J.M. "Introduction: The Life and Thought of Joachim Wach," in J.M. Kitagawa, ed., *The Comparative Study of Religions* by Joachim Wach (Posthumous publication). New York: Columbia University Press, 1958.

_____. *Gibt es ein Verstehen Fremder Religionen?* Leiden: E.J. Brill, 1963.

_____. *Religion in Japanese History.* New York: Columbia University Press, 1966.

_____. "Gohei Hasami: A Rite of Purification of Time at Mt. Koya," *Proceedings of the 9th Congress of the International Association for the History of Religions*, Vol. II. Leiden: E.J. Brill, 1968.

_____. *Religions of the East.* Philadelphia: Westminster, 1968.

_____. "Early Shinto," in Honko, L., ed., *Science of Religion: Studies in Methodology.* The Hague: Mouton, 1979.

_____. "The 1893 World's Parliament of Religions and Its Legacy." Chicago: The University of Chicago, Divinity School, 1984.

_____. "Random Reflections on Methodological Problems of the History of Religions," in Tyloch, W., ed., *Current Progress in the Methodology of the Science of Religions.* Warsaw: Polish Scientific Publishers, 1984.

_____. *Gendai-sekai to Shūkyō-gaku.* Tokyo: Shinkyō Shuppansha, 1985.

_____. *On Understanding Japanese Religion.* Princeton: Princeton University Press, 1987.

Kitagawa, J.M., ed. *Modern Trends in World Religions.* La Salle: The Open Court, 1959.

Kitagawa, J.M., ed. *The History of Religions: Essays on the Problem of Understanding.* Chicago: The University of Chicago Press, 1967.

Kitagawa, J.M., ed. *Understanding and Believing: Essays by Joachim Wach.* New York: Harper, 1968.

Kitagawa, J.M., ed. *Understanding Modern China.* Chicago: Quadrangle Books, 1969.

Kitagawa, J.M., ed. *American Refugee Policy: Some Ethical and Religious Reflections.* Minneapolis: Winston Press, 1984.

Kitagawa, J.M., ed. *The History of Religions: Retrospect and Prospect.* New York: Macmillan, 1985.

Kitagawa, J.M. and C.H. Long, eds. *Myths and Symbols: Studies in Honor of Mircea Eliade.* Chicago: The University of Chicago Press, 1969.

Kitagawa, J.M. and F.E. Reynolds. "Theravada Buddhism in the Twentieth Century," in Dumoulin, H. & J.C. Maraldo, eds., *Buddhism in the Modern World.* New York: Macmillan, 1976.

Konvitz, Milton R. *The Alien and the Asiatic in American Law.* Ithaca: Cornell University Press, 1946.

Kramer, Hendrik. *The Christian Message in a Non-Christian World.* London: The Edinburgh House, 1938.

_____. *World Cultures and World Religions.* Philadelphia: Westminster, 1960.

Lach, Donald F. *Asia in the Making of Europe*, 2 vols. Chicago: The University of Chicago Press, 1965.

Latourette, K.S. *The Chinese: Their History and Culture*, 2 vols. New York: Macmillan, 1934.

Leeuw, G. van der. *Religion in Essence and Manifestation.* London: G. Allen & Unwin, 1938.

Lin, Yutang, ed. and tr. *The Wisdom of Confucius.* New York: Random House, 1938.

Lubac, Henri de. *La recontre du Buddhisme et de l'Occident.* Paris: Aubier Editions Montaigne, 1952.

MacNair, H.F., ed. *China.* Berkeley: University of California Press, 1946.

Manglapus, Raul S. "Philippine Culture and Modernization," in Bellah, R.N., ed. *Religion and Progress in Modern Asia.* New York: The Free Press, 1965.

Manikam, R.B., ed. *Christianity and the Asian Revolution.* New York: Friendship Press, 1954.

Matsumoto, Shigeru. *Motoori Norinaga 1730-1801.* Cambridge: Harvard University Press, 1970.

Mead, Sidney E. "Christendom, Religion and American Revolution," in Brauer, J.C., ed., *Religion and American Revolution.* Philadelphia: Fortress, 1976.

Morgenthau, H.J. *In Defense of the National Interest.* New York: A.A. Knopf, 1951.

Muilenburg, J. "The Ethics of the Prophet," in Anshen, R.N., ed. *Moral Principles of Action*. New York: Harper, 1952.

Muller, H.J. *The Use of the Past: Profiles of Former Societies*. New York: The New American Library of World Literature: A Mentor Book, 1952.

Murti, T.R.V. *The Central Philosophy of Buddhism*. London: G. Allen & Unwin, 1955.

Myrdal, Gunnar. *Asian Drama: An Inquiry into the Poverty of Nations*, 3 vols. New York: Pantheon, 1968.

Nakane, Chie. *Japanese Society*. Berkeley: University of California Press, 1972.

Needham, Joseph. *Science and Civilization in China*. London: Cambridge University Press, 1956.

Nehru, J. *Jawaharal Nehru's Speeches*. New Delhi: Government of India, Publication Division, 1949.

_____. *The Discovery of India*. New York: John Day, 1956.

Neill, Stephen. *The Christian Society*. New York: Harper, 1952.

Neill, Stephen, et. al., eds. *Concise Dictionary of the Christian Mission*. Nashville: Abingdon Press, 1971.

Nevin, A.J. "Patronato Real," in Neill, S., et. al., eds., *Concise Dictionary of the Christian Mission*. Nashville: Abingdon Press, 1971.

Nihon Gakujutsu Shinkokai, tr. *The Manyōshū*. New York: Columbia University Press, 1965.

Nikhilananda, Swami. "Hindu Ethics," in R.N. Anshen, ed., *Moral Principles of Action*. New York: Harper, 1952.

Nitobe Inazo ct. al. *Western Influences in Modern Japan*. Chicago: The University of Chicago Press, 1931.

Northrop, F.S.C. *The Meeting of East and West*. New York: Macmillan, 1946.

_____. *The Taming of the Nations*. New York: Macmillan, 1952.

Panikkar, K.M. *Asia and Western Domination*. London: G. Allen & Unwin, 1953.

Parsons, Talcott. "Christianity," in *The International Encyclopedia of the Social Sciences*. New York: Macmillan, 1968.

Radhakrishna, S. and P.T. Raju, eds. *The Concept of Man*. London: G. Allen & Unwin, 1960.

Rahman, Fazlur. *Major Themes of the Qur'ān*. Minneapolis: Bibliotheca Islamica, 1980.

Romulo, C.P. "A Policy for the West in Asia." *Saturday Review of Literature*, XXXIV, 31 (August 4), 1951.

Rostow, W.W. with R.W. Hatch. *An American Policy in Asia*. New York: John Wileym, 1955.

Roy, Sjit. "A Marxist View of Liberation," in Samartha, S.J., ed. *Living Faiths and Ultimate Goals*. Geneve: W.C.C., 1974.

Sakisyanz, E. *Buddhist Background of the Burmese Revolution*. The Hague: Martinus Niihoff, 1965.

Sansom, G.B. *Japan: A Short Cultural History.* New York: D. Appleton-Century, 1943.

_____. *The Western World and Japan.* New York: A.A. Knopf, 1962.

Scheiner, Irwin. *Christian Converts and Social Protest in Meiji Japan.* Berkeley: University of California Press, 1970.

Schimmel, Annemarie. *And Muhammad Is His Messenger.* Chapel Hill: The University of North Carolina Press, 1985.

Sen, Amulyachandra. *Asoka's Edicts.* Calcutta: The Indian Publicity Society, 1956.

Smith, Reuben W., ed. *Islamic Civilization in the Middle East.* Chicago: The University of Chicago, Committee on Near Eastern Studies, 1965.

Soedjatmoko. "Cultural Motivations to Progress: The 'Exterior' and the 'Interior Views.' " In Bellah, R.N., ed. *Religion and Progress in Modern Asia.* New York: The Free Press, 1965.

Spae, Joseph, CICM, ed. *China Update.* Belgium: Oud-Heverlee.

Spengler, Oswald. *The Decline of the West,* 2 vols. New York: A.A. Knopf, 1930.

Stevenson, Adlai. *Call to Greatness.* New York: Harper, 1954.

Suzuki, D.T. *Zen and Japanese Culture.* New York: Pantheon Books, Bollingen Series, LXIV, 1959.

Sweet, W.W. "Christianity in the Americas," in A.C. Baker, ed. *A Short History of Christianity.* Chicago: The University of Chicago Press, 1940.

Takeuchi, Yoshinori. "Modern Japanese Philosophy," *Encyclopaedia Britannica*, XVII, 1966.

Teggart, F. *Rome and China: A Study of Correlations in Historical Events*. Berkeley: University of California Press, 1939.

ten Broek, Jacobus, et. al. *Prejudice, War, and the Constitution*. Berkeley: University of California Press, 1954.

Thompson, L.C. *Chinese Religion: An Introduction*. Belmont: Dickenson, 1969.

Toynbee, A.J. *Civilization on Trial*. New York: Oxford University Press, 1948.

_____. *The World and the West*. New York: Oxford University Press, 1953.

Tsunoda, Ryūsaku, et. al., compls. *Sources of Japanese Tradition*. New York: Columbia University Press, 1958.

Warner, Langdon. *The Enduring Art of Japan*. Cambridge: Harvard University Press, 1952.

Wierszowski, Helene. *The Medieval University*. Princeton: D. Van Norstrand, 1966.

Yuasa, Yasuo. *The Body: Toward an Eastern Mind-Body Theory*. Albany: SUNY Press, 1987.

Zeine, Z.N. *Arab-Turkish Relations and the Emergence of Arab Nationalism*. Beirut: Khayat, 1958.

B. Journal and Newspaper Articles

Bartlett, Vernon. "Opening of Bandung Conference." *Manchester Guardian*, Air Ed., April 21, 1955.

Benz, Ernst. "The Theological Meaning of the History of Religions." *The Journal of Religion*, XLI:1, January 1961.

Bernard, J.A. "A Maturation Crisis in India: The V.P. Singh Experiment." *Asian Survey*, XXVII, No. 4, April 1987.

Cameron, M.E. "Far Eastern Studies in the U.S." *The Far Eastern Quarterly*, VII:2, February 1948.

Chu, Yu-Kuang. "The Liberal Values of Non-Western Studies." *TOPIC: The Journal of the Liberal Arts.* Washington, PA: Washington & Jefferson College, 1962.

"On Communism." *The Reporter*, January 27, 1955.

Cousins, Norman. "Talk with the PM." *Saturday Review*, May 27, 1961, pp. 10-33.

"Faculty News." *Criterion*, XXIV, Autumn, 1985.

Doi, M. "Dialogue between Living Faiths in Japan." *Japanese Religions*, VI, No. 3, August 1970, pp. 49-73.

Drummond, Roscoe. "China's Game in Africa." *Chicago Sun-Times*, May 20, 1965.

Federspiel, H.M. "Islam and Development in the Nations of ASEAN." *Asian Survey*, XXV, No. 8, August, 1945, pp. 805-821.

Gup, Ted. "The Gang of One Million." *Chicago Sun-Times*, December 30, 1986.

Heisig, J.W. "Facing Religious Pluralism in Asia." *Inter-Religio*, No. 4, Fall 1983.

Isaacs, H.R. "The Dimension of the Crisis." *Saturday Review of Literature*, XXXIV, 31, August 4, 1951.

King, W.L. Mackenzie, quoted in *Chicago Sun-Times*, Saturday, January 3, 1976.

Kitagawa, J.M. "This Cannot Happen Again!" *Living Church*, CXI, November 1945.

_____. "Sanka-gaijin-gakusha no yokogao." *Gakujutsu Geppō* (Japanese Scientific Monthly), XI, October 1958, pp. 448-452.

_____. "Search for Self-Identity: Asian Peoples Today." *Divinity School News*, XXVI, November 1959, pp. 10-32.

_____. "East and West – A Dialogue." *Perspectives* (South Bend, Notre Dame University Press), Vol. VI, Jan.-Feb., 1961.

_____. "Koteki Hakase" (Dr. Hu Shih). *Tokyo Mainichi*, March, 1962.

_____. "Asia Revisited." *Criterion*, Summer, 1962, pp. 31-35.

_____. "The Japanese *Kokutai* [National Community]: History and Myth." *History of Religions*, 13:3, February 1974.

_____. "One of Many Faces of China: Maoism as a Quasi-Religion." *Japanese Journal of Religious Studies*, I, Nos. 2-3, June-Sept., 1974, pp. 125-141.

_____. "Reality and Illusion: Some Characteristics of the Early Japanese 'World of Meaning.' " *Journal of Oriental Society of Australia*, II, 1976.

_____. "Humanistic and Theological History of Religions." *NUMEN*, XXVII, December 1980, pp. 199-219.

_____. "Glimpse of China." *Criterion*, XXI, Spring 1982.

Kristol, Irving. "The 20th Century Began in 1945." *New York Times Magazine*, May 2, 1965.

Lippman, Walter. "Our Involvement in Asia's Crisis." *Chicago Sun-Times*, November 1, 1962.

Mancall, Mark. Review of *Formosa Betrayed* by H. Kerr (New York: Houghton Mifflin, 1965). *Book Week*, January 23, 1966.

Mansergh, N. "The Impact of Asian Membership." *The Listener*, December 8, 1954.

Nehru's statement reported in *Manchester Guardian*, December 23, 1954.

Panikkar, K.M. & C.P. Fitzgerald on "The Bandung Conference." *The Nation*, 180:14, April 2, 1955.

Qayyaum, A. "The Role of Islam in Asia." *Saturday Review of Literature*, XXXIV, 31, August 4, 1951.

Reischauer, Edwin O. "Must Korea Be Another Vietnam?" *Chicago Sun-Times*, Sunday, June 22, 1975, Section I, p. 3.

Schilp, P.A. "Some Call Him God...Gandhi in Retrospect." *Chicago Sun-Times*, February 16, 1958.

Stevenson, Adlai, quoted in *Chicago Sun-Times*, Sept. 18, 1953.

Toynbee, A.J. "The Outlook for the West Today." *Motive*, December, 1961.

Turner, R.E. "The Nature of the Crisis." *Saturday Review of Literature*, XXXIV, 31, August 4, 1951.

Will, George F. "Korea, Where 54,246 GIs Died for a Tie." *Chicago Sun-Times*, Sunday, June 22, 1975, Section I-A, p. 3.

Win Maung, U. Statement read at the Sixth Conference of Buddhists, Autumn, 1961 at Phnom Penh, Cambodia.

Previously Published Books
in the Rockwell Lecture Series

The Structure of Christian Ethics Joseph Sittler

Religion and American Democracy Roy F. Nichols

Biblical Thought and the Secular University George Arthur Buttrick

Darwin and the Modern World View John C. Greene

The Lost Image of Man Julian N. Hartt

The Moral Issue in Statecraft: Twentieth-Century Approaches and Problems Kenneth W. Thompson

Archaeology, Historical Analogy, and Early Biblical Tradition William F. Albright

On New Creation B.D. Napier

The American Search for Soul Robert S. Michaelsen

Other Works by J.M. Kitagawa

(Excluding German, French, Portugese, Japanese, Chinese and Korean translations of some works)

Author:
Religions of the East (1960: Rev. Ed., 1968)
Gibt es ein Verstehen fremder Religionen? (1963)
Religion in Japanese History (1965)
Gendai-Sekai to Shūkyō-gaku (Contemporary World and "Religionswissenschaft") (1985)
On Understanding Japanese Religion (1987)
The History of Religions: Understanding Human Experience (1988)
The Quest for Human Unity (1990)

Translator:
(With Wing-tsit Chan, I.R. Al Fārūquī and P.T. Raju) *The Great Asian Religions: An Anthology* (1969)

Editor:
The Comparative Study of Religions (The Posthumous work of J. Wach; 1958)
Modern Trends in World Religions (1959)
The History of Religions: Essays on the Problem of Understanding (1967)
Understanding and Believing (The Posthumous work of J. Wach; 1968)
Understanding Modern China (1969)
American Refugee Policy: Ethical and Religious Reflections (1984)
The History of Religions: Retrospect and Prospect (1985)
The Religious Traditions of Asia (1989)
Religious Studies, Theological Studies and the University-Divinity School (1991)

Co-editor:

(With M. Eliade), *The History of Religions: Essays in Methodology* (1959)

(With A.L. Miller), *Folk Religion in Japan* (The Haskell Lectures by I. Hori; 1968)

(With C.H. Long), *Myths and Symbols: Studies in Honor of M. Eliade* (1969)

(With G. Alles), *Introduction to the History of Religions* (Translations of J. Wach's *Religionswissenschaft* and Other Essays; 1987)

(With G. Alles), *Essays in the History of Religions* (by J. Wach, 1968)

(With Mark Cummings), *Buddhism and Asian History* (1989)

(With Nakamura Hajime and Masutani Fumio), *Kindai Bukkyō Meicho-Zenshū* ("Collected Works of Modern Buddhism"; 8 vols., 1960-66)

(With M. Eliade, Editor-in-Chief, 9 Editors, Associate and Assistant Editors), *Encyclopedia of Religion* (16 vols., 1987)